BOOKS BY GERI HARRINGTON

The Salad Book (*1977*)
Summer Garden, Winter Kitchen (*1976*)
The College Cookbook (*1973*)

THE SALAD BOOK

THE
SALAD
BOOK

From Seed to Salad Bowl

GERI HARRINGTON

New York   ATHENEUM   1977

Library of Congress Cataloging in Publication Data

Harrington, Geri.
  The salad book.

  Includes indexes.
  1. Salad greens.   2. Vegetable gardening.
3. Salads.   I. Title.
SB321.H28   1977   641.3'5   76-53406
ISBN 0-689-10789-7

COMPOSITION BY AMERICAN BOOK—STRATFORD PRESS, INC.
SADDLE BROOK, NEW JERSEY
PRINTED AND BOUND BY THE BOOK PRESS, BRATTLEBORO, VERMONT
DESIGNED BY KATHLEEN CAREY
FIRST EDITION

FOR TY

CONTENTS

PART I

THE SALAD GARDEN

INTRODUCTION

How to Grow Chicken Salad

L E T M E S A Y right off, I'm not going to tell you.

For a first-class chicken salad, you would need chicken, celery, pimientos, shallots, capers, at least one kind of lettuce, eggs and olive oil (for homemade mayonnaise), salt, and pepper. This book won't tell you how to raise chickens or olive trees, but it will tell you how to grow almost everything else for the salad.

Which brings me to a decision I had to make in writing this book—what should I leave out? It was easy enough to decide to omit directions for raising chickens and pigs or building a lobster pond, but it was hard to draw the line in the vegetable garden.

In my book *Summer Garden, Winter Kitchen,* I told you how to grow and cook twenty-one root vegetables. I have a clear conscience about leaving gardening directions for most of them out of *this* book, although I have included the vegetables themselves in some new salad recipes.

In addition, however, there are vegetables like eggplant and zucchini, which make marvelous cold Turkish, Russian, and Persian dishes. I included them in the recipe section but not in the garden section. The garden section covers tomatoes, almost all the salad greens (old and new), vegetables like carrots, bean sprouts, and cucumbers, and a few herbs. I hope you think I made the right decision about what to omit.

Using This Book—Where to Find the Information You Need

How to Use a Seed Catalog (Chapter I). As far as I know, this chapter is a first; at least, I don't know of any other garden book that tells you how to use a seed catalog. Although seed catalogs are very attractive and crammed with useful information, they are traps for the unwary, a hopeless hodgepodge of superlatives for the average gardener. Here are the things you need to know in order to read a catalog with understanding.

Most seedsmen are eminently reliable; all are very helpful in personal correspondence. However, this chapter will help you to plan your garden and to write up an order that will make your garden plan a reality.

How to Use the Guide and Glossary (Chapter II). Most garden books have individual chapters on soil preparation, fertilizing, and the other tasks necessary before seeds can be planted. I have tried to put all this information into a more usable form, so you don't have to wade through things you already know to locate the one fact you need to check out.

With the format of the Glossary, you can look up whatever you are specifically concerned with. It tells you practically everything you need to know, from Acid Soil to Winter Hardy, and the cross references make it unnecessary for you to know the exact technical term for your information.

It will be helpful, also, when you come upon directions you don't understand. In an earlier book, for instance, I spoke of a vegetable "bolting." No one, including the proofreader, seemed to know what it meant, although it is used in every garden seed catalog written for the general public. Since it is a short, as well as technically accurate, way of saying a plant is going to seed (which you don't want it to do unless you are growing seeds), it is useful to know what it means. Selecting a lettuce that a seed catalog describes as "slow-bolting" can mean the difference between a delicious lettuce crop and inedible plants taking up valuable space in the garden. The Glossary makes it easy and convenient to look up this sort of word without putting down your garden book to hunt for the dictionary.

Guide to Varieties. At the end of gardening instructions for each vegetable, I have suggested some specific varieties for you to try. Confronted with eighty varieties (as in the Stokes catalog listing for tomatoes), even the most seasoned gardener might feel overwhelmed. I hope these recommendations will help you thread your way through the maze.

If, in spite of all my good intentions, you feel I have left out some absolutely essential information, do write and tell me so I can do better next time. I would also very much appreciate it if you would share with me any of your experiences, good or bad. If we all help one another, we will, perhaps, one day grow superlative and super-productive gardens—it couldn't help but make a better world!

GERI HARRINGTON
Wilton, Connecticut

CHAPTER ONE

How to Read a Seed Catalog

SEED CATALOGS ARE a gold mine of information for the knowledgeable gardener. Like most mines, however, the ore is not just lying on the surface but has to be dug out. Also, since every seed offered has some merit (or it wouldn't be in the catalog in the first place), it is necessary for you to decipher the superlatives to find the variety that is right for you. But to start at the beginning.

Why Order Seeds by Mail?

Since almost every hardware store, supermarket, and nursery has racks and racks of vegetable and flower seeds, it may seem unnecessarily time-consuming and unwieldy to order from a seed catalog. After all, first you have to send for the catalog, then you have to peruse it, and finally there is all the bother of filling in the order forms, making out the check, and, worst of all, waiting patiently for your order to arrive.

Buying seeds from a rack is instant gratification. The packet, with a glowing picture of the vegetable, is right in front of you. Planting and growing directions, even a hardiness-zone map, are on the back (and they are good, too). You browse happily, spinning the rack to make sure you haven't missed anything, and make your selection judiciously. It's great for impulse buying. In no time, your list of beans, beets, and lettuce is augmented by ageratum, portulaca, and a green zinnia that looks new and really wild. These extra seeds sometimes end up in your garden, but more often you find they won't fit in anywhere and you put them away for next year along with last year's impulse purchases.

When you choose seeds from the rack, you are usually confronted with several varieties of each vegetable. It looks like a wide choice and they all sound great; the pictures are what usually influence your final choice. What you may not realize is that *the selection may not include any of the superior hybrid or out-of-the-ordinary varieties;* racks are geared to a mass market, and hybrid seeds are comparatively expensive—but they are expensive for a good reason and they may be well worth it to you.

In addition, the packets seem inexpensive; they are often not, really, because *they may contain very few seeds compared to a packet for the same price from a seed catalog.* This doesn't always matter, because the average home gardener can't use all the seeds in a packet anyhow; on the other hand, if it is a vegetable like beans, radishes, lettuce, or spinach, which you will be planting several times during the season, it is poor economy to buy several small packets instead of the larger quantities available by mail.

And this is another point. *Seed packets in the store usually come in only one size packet;* by mail you can order by the packet, or from ½ ounce on up (depending on the vegetable).

For what varieties you are offered, for the quantity of seeds per packet, for wider selection, you will do better almost every time ordering by mail. Of course if you can't, do the best you can with the racks; if you check out the catalogs first, you will at least know which varieties to buy among the ones available.

Caution: if you buy from store racks, beware of last year's seeds. The better seed companies now date their seed packets; look before you buy. If you cannot find a date on the packet, try another store. While many seeds are viable for two, three, or even more years, *many are not.* Anyhow, why shouldn't you be the one to get the benefit of this keeping quality (in case you don't use all the seeds the year you buy them)?

The catalogs carry the latest developments in varieties; buying from seed racks limits your horizon. If you want to experiment with ruby lettuce, ornamental kale, or vegetable spaghetti (a kind of squash), you won't find them in store racks until they've been around for a while. Racks specialize in ordinary best-sellers. I never met a vegetable I didn't like (once I learned to grow and cook parsnips), but I also like to keep trying new ones. Many of the old varieties are sitting ducks for pests and diseases that new varieties have been bred to resist.

Another advantage to catalogs is that you can make your choices comfortably at home with your feet up in front of a roaring fire, or in businesslike efficiency at your desk with a rough garden plan in front of you. As you compare catalogs, pictures, and offerings, you find yourself choosing more and more judiciously. And you learn a lot from reading over the catalog. Which brings us to our next point.

How to Choose the Best Types

Let's look at two good catalogs, Burpee and Harris. In both, cabbages rate two pages. Both give general information on how to grow cabbages, including when to plant. The information they give, though, is quite different otherwise. Burpee's tells you how large an area a packet of seeds will sow; Harris explains about insect control, with specific recommendations. There is very little overlapping and much interesting reading.

Burpee divides cabbages into six categories; Harris into five:

Burpee	*Harris*
Earliest Cabbage	Early Cabbage
Chinese or Celery Cabbage	Midseason and Danish Cabbage
Early Cabbage	Red Cabbage
Late Fall or Winter Cabbage	Savoy Cabbage
Savoy Cabbage	Chinese Cabbage
Red Cabbage	

Actually they both carry cabbages for all seasons; they just categorize them differently.

If the type is a little unusual, as with Chinese cabbage, each catalog tells you a little extra about it; what it tastes like, how to prepare it—you are encouraged to try it.

If, in looking over the categories, you don't know the difference between, say, ordinary cabbage and savoy cabbage, check it out at your supermarket.

There are illustrations of many, but not all, the types. In Burpee's, all illustrations are in color; in Harris many are not. The Harris cabbage photographs are, as it happens, black-and-white. This is not the disadvantage it might seem; as any photographer knows, color can confuse and keep the eye from really "seeing" the object. The Burpee cabbage pictures are good, especially the one for savoy, but the Harris pictures give you a much better idea of how a type will look in your garden, and this helps visualize a good garden plan. Harris also shows you what Chinese cabbage looks like—a big help if you've never seen any.

In choosing among the various types, you should take into

consideration days to maturity, time of year you plan to plant *and to harvest,* amount of space needed between plants and between rows, uses (some varieties are especially good for storage or preserving) , and, of course, disease resistance.

How to Choose Varieties

Here you enter an endlessly fascinating world. If you wanted to, you could grow a whole garden of just cabbages or carrots or radishes; there are so many different varieties of each vegetable. However, since that is not practical for most gardeners, here are some suggestions.

Still using our cabbage as an example, we find that the two firms list varieties not found in each other's catalogs. In some cases, this is because it is a hybrid developed by that seedsman —as is the case with MARKET PRIZE, a Harris hybrid, or COPENHAGEN MARKET, a Burpee hybrid. Sometimes the same variety will be listed in almost any catalog you pick up, as is the case with EARLY JERSEY WAKEFIELD.

Obviously you aren't going to go wrong choosing a variety that is so good every catalog lists it. You aren't going to grow anything unusual, either; it's all up to you and what you want in your garden.

It's interesting to compare the listings for EARLY JERSEY WAKEFIELD. Harris characterizes this as "Early, Delicious . . . 64 days. For really tender, mild cabbage, grow Jersey Wakefield. It matures quickly yet will stand well without splitting and a few successive plantings provide a continuous supply from your garden all season. The plants are small and the heads are of conical shape, pointed on top and rounded at the base. The flavor is delicious, mild and sweet, far superior to the harder, roundheaded cabbage in our opinion." They offer it in various quantities from a packet to $1/4$ pound. There is a good illustration.

Burpee puts it more succinctly: "Yellows-Resistant. 63 days.

Small pointed heads 7 in. deep with especially fine flavor; crisp and tender. Weight 2 to 3 lbs. each." And offers one ounce as its largest quantity.

Let's see what you've learned if you've read these listings carefully:

1. "Yellows" is a cabbage disease. (Check with your county agent to see if it is a problem in your area.)
2. Sometimes cabbages "split," and it's better if they don't.
3. Not all cabbages are mild in flavor.
4. Cabbages vary in the shape of their heads.
5. Hard, roundheaded cabbages are not the most delicately delicious.
6. Not all cabbages lend themselves to successive plantings.
7. Some cabbages are bigger, therefore take up more garden space than others.
8. Some cabbages have to be picked as soon as they mature. (They don't "stand well.")

That's a lot of information from reading just two descriptions of one variety of cabbage. Since Burpee lists twenty varieties as against Harris's fourteen, they cannot give any single variety as much room as Harris can. Between the two, however, you can learn a lot about cabbages.

You've come this far, but how do you choose among EARLY JERSEY WAKEFIELD, GOLDEN ACRE 84, and MARKET TOPPER from Harris; or COPENHAGEN MARKET, EARLIANA, EMERALD CROSS HYBRID, GOLDEN ACRE, MARION MARKET, STONEHEAD HYBRID, and STEIN'S FLAT DUTCH from Burpee? As we have indicated earlier, you can take the easy way out and choose JERSEY WAKE-FIELD. GOLDEN ACRE is listed in both catalogs, but Harris has a plus; their 84 strain is "the best GOLDEN ACRE to grow, we believe. Ready as early as the standard strains, its round, attractive heads have shorter cores and better interior structure."

Sounds convincing and, from a seedsman as reputable as Harris, reliable. They do add, however, "not long-standing but it will hold better than some extra-early varieties." This is very important information. If it is not long-standing, you will have to pick it all at once. If you don't want to have to eat cabbage every day for a week or however long your heads hold out, then don't choose this one. Also, you gather from this description that *all* very early cabbages are not long-standing; unless this is what you want, don't plant any of them, or plant only a few.

Burpee doesn't come right out and say their earliest cabbages are not long-standing; if you read carefully, they don't say they are, either. Whereas, with some of their other varieties they do. Very often omissions are an important clue. They may be due to lack of room, but generally you can assume that if some of the qualities important to that particular vegetable—slow-bolting for lettuce, for example—are omitted, that variety would not be your best choice.

Tips

As a home gardener, you don't have to worry about how your vegetables will travel or stand up under the rigorous demands of modern distribution methods. In order to meet supermarket demands for vegetables that will arrive in good condition after cross-country shipping, and stand up well in the produce department, growers have developed special varieties that will take all kinds of punishment.

The qualities that make a good traveler don't necessarily contribute to flavor, tenderness, and good eating in general. For instance, the reason you almost never see raspberries for sale is that they refuse to grow according to these requirements; they insist on staying hard to pick, delicate to handle, and poor shippers; no amount of experimenting has produced a tough, rugged raspberry—thank goodness.

If a catalog says something like "whether for home or market use" or "acclaimed by commercial growers," go on to something else. Burpee doesn't put it that way; "fine for home gardens" is your clue to a variety you won't find in the market. *Grow the special, extra-delicious vegetables you can't buy; they are usually by far the best.*

Watch for special notations in the descriptions of varieties. *Tomato names, for example, are often followed by the initials V, VF, or VFN.* This is absolutely essential information. V stands for verticillium resistant, F for fusarium wilt resistant, N for root-knot nematode resistant. These are the three most serious diseases tomatoes are prone to: they can completely destroy your crop. If you can't resist beefsteak and some of the other wonderful old types of tomatoes, at least hedge your bets by planting the disease-resistant strains. It takes a lot of work and worry out of gardening. H after a variety is not a disease; it means it is a hybrid.

Many vegetables cannot be started in the open garden because their growing season is too long; tomatoes, eggplants, and peppers are among these. You can start them in the house or buy the plants from local nurseries. If you are planning to start your own, the name of each variety is followed (in seed catalogs) by a number; *this tells you the number of days to maturity.* There is, however, something many gardeners who have been ordering these seeds for years do not realize; it is the number of days to maturity *from the time the plants are set out in the open garden.* To get the actual length of time from seed germination to maturity, add on how long it takes seeds to reach the open-garden seedling stage. You may have your mouth all ready for a juicy tomato a month too early if you think Burpee's BIG GIRL HYBRID VF will be ready to eat in 78 days (the way it says in the catalog).

CHAPTER TWO

The How-to-Grow-Vegetables Guide and Glossary

THIS CHAPTER CONTAINS, in alphabetical order, the information that usually appears in gardening books in lengthy chapters on Choosing the Garden Site, Soil Preparation, pH and What to Do About It, and so forth and is not covered later on under specific directions for individual vegetables. This format will, it is hoped, make it easy to find exactly the information you want without making you wade through a lot of information you already know or don't need at the moment.

No matter how knowledgeable a gardener is, there are times when he wants to check something out or refresh his memory; a glossary is quick, easy reference.

Another advantage is that it allows me to be succinct; without leaving out essentials, I have tried to keep explanations as short as possible. Gardeners are busy people and this is meant to save them time.

ACID SOIL Below pH 7.0 in the pH scale, which runs from 0 to 14. Some vegetables, such as potatoes, do better in a slightly acid soil; some, such as beets, are intolerant of acidity and require a more basic or alkaline soil. Only a soil analysis (*see* Soil Test) can tell you what your soil is. It is easily changed or corrected to whatever pH your crops require. To make an acid soil more alkaline, add ground limestone.

AERATION The process of supplying air to soil. Plants require soil with a certain amount of oxygen in it. One of the problems created by overwatering is the elimination of sufficient oxygen, so plants suffocate. Incorporating plenty of humus and organic material helps to keep your soil light and fluffy, with good drainage, so that danger of waterlogging is minimized.

ALKALINE SOIL Above pH 7.0 in the pH scale. The opposite of acid soil. If your soil is too alkaline, incorporate peat moss, which will both condition and correct the alkalinity.

ANNUAL For all practical purposes, any plant that should be planted anew from seed each year. Some plants that are naturally perennial become annuals in cold climates, because they are not winter hardy. Many perennials do better if treated like annuals—that is to say, if you let them, they will winter over and come up themselves the following spring—but you will get better results if you dig them up, store them over the winter, and replant in the spring. Shallots are a good example of this type of vegetable. These are not to be confused with annual plants, like cherry tomatoes, that self-seed so easily you might almost think they were perennials.

ARTIFICIAL FERTILIZERS *See* Chemical Fertilizers.

BACTERIA *See* Soil Bacteria.

BEDDING PLANTS A term that has come to mean any plant that keeps a compact shape so that it makes a neat area in a bed—similar to edging plants, except that edging plants tend to be low-growing whereas bedding plants could be cushion mums, for example. Lettuce, parsley, and many other vegetables make excellent decorative bedding plants.

BOLTING Going to seed. Vegetables such as spinach and lettuce that prefer cool growing weather will suddenly start to form seed when the weather turns hot. Since seed formation spoils the plant for eating purposes, varieties of lettuce and spinach that are described as "slow-bolting" are generally considered more desirable.

BORON A trace element necessary to healthy plants. If soil is deficient in boron, your celery stems may crack and your beets be disappointing. If you use organic fertilizers such as granite dust, you will automatically get enough boron.

CALCIUM A mineral necessary to healthy plants. In the form of limestone, it conditions the soil and makes it alkaline. Wood ashes, bone mcal, eggshells, and seashells are also excellent sources of calcium.

CHELATES Substances that compound with metals to make them more readily available to plants. The name means "clawlike," an indication of how they lock onto minerals. Most familiar type is iron chelate, which restores green to leaves that have yellowed owing to lack of iron—particularly noticeable in acid-loving plants like andromeda. Manure acts as a chelate with phosphate; all soil bacteria have some chelating action. Seaweed used as fertilizer has a very beneficial chelating action.

CHEMICAL FERTILIZERS Also called artificial or inorganic fertilizers. They are man-made, often from petroleum. Chemical fertilizers supply needed nutrients to plants but at the expense of the soil; they destroy soil bacteria, giving them nothing to feed on, and appear to be hostile to earthworms, which tend to disappear from soil regularly treated with chemical fertilizers. Recent studies have shown that crops grown with inorganic fertilizers are not as nutritive as those grown organically. (*See* Fertilizer.) Chemical fertilizers are quickly depleted by plants and need to be constantly replenished.

CLAY SOIL Soil in which the original rock particles have broken down too completely and are too fine. When wet, it forms a compact ball that will not crumble when broken. It is difficult to cultivate, water, or plant in early spring.

Clay soil is especially unsuited to root crops or any crop requiring a deep root, such as endive. In general, it is undesirable for all vegetables.

Fortunately, clay soil can be changed to more satisfactory loamy soil (in a small area such as a home garden) by the addition of humus, greensand, granite dust, lime, and similar materials.

COLD FRAME A protected, covered outdoor area, partially in the ground, for starting seeds earlier than normal soil and weather conditions would permit. Can be bought ready-made or easily constructed. May be unheated or heated with electric wires. If heated, it is technically called a hotbed.

COMPOST Organic material that has been broken down by soil bacteria into rich, humusy material that will both condition and fertilize the soil. Any organic matter—potato and other vegetable peelings, coffee grounds, grass clippings, leaves, eggshells—will turn into compost. It is not advisable to incorporate meat scraps into a compost heap, because they will attract all the meat-eating animals in the area— including your neighbors' dogs.

COMPOST HEAP The true gold mine of the organic gardener. The difference between a garbage dump and a compost heap lies in the management of the organic refuse. Compost heaps are layer cakes of organic matter, manure or fertilizer, and earth; they should be kept moist with an occasional wetting down with the hose, and turned over regularly or aerated.

Compost heaps do not have any unpleasant odor; they are usually contained on three sides by fencing or wooden boards in an unobtrusive corner where they can be reached by a hose.

Every good organic gardener has his own favorite method of handling a compost heap; there are many books on the subject and each one extolls its own method. Compost is one of the best examples in modern times of successful, worthwhile recycling and is a money-saver as well.

CORNELL MIX A soil mixture developed at Cornell University that consists of peat moss, vermiculite, and fertilizers. It is ideal for container gardening, and if used for starting seeds, reduces the necessity for fertilizing in the early stages, as well as furnishing more support for the plant than does vermiculite.

You can buy it commercially under such names as Pro-Mix, Jiffy Mix, and Redi-Earth, or you can make your own.

COTTONSEED MEAL An excellent organic source of nitrogen.

CROP ROTATION Changing the garden plan each year so that vegetables are not planted in the same place two consecutive years.

Since different vegetables have different nutritive requirements, planting a vegetable like tomatoes, for instance, in the same spot year after year depletes the soil more quickly than if they were rotated with lettuce or peas.

Another reason for crop rotation is that diseases and pests which may have wintered over, and even multiplied, are all set to attack last year's crop; root maggots ready for another crop of carrots will be foiled by the tomatoes you plant instead.

Ideally, crop rotation repeats a crop in the same location once every three years.

My garden is too small for this kind of jigsaw-puzzle planning, so I fertilize extra heavily when repeating a crop —especially with those nutrients that I know a particular crop requires. So far, I have been lucky, but rotating crops is obviously desirable if you can do it.

CULTIVATE To prepare the soil for planting. Before seeding, to cultivate includes rototilling and spading; after seeding, the soil is usually disturbed just on the surface to keep a crust from forming, to kill weeds, and to incorporate fertilizer into the top two or three inches.

How deep you cultivate prior to planting depends on your facilities and what you are planting, but it is important that in the process you never bring the subsoil up over the topsoil even if you want to disturb the subsoil.

Do not cultivate too early in the spring or the soil will compact. Vegetables that can be planted "as soon as the soil can be worked" can be planted as soon as you have been able to rototill.

Mulching eliminates the need for cultivating after seeding, and some long-time organic gardeners don't even bother to cultivate before seeding.

DAMPING-OFF The apparently mysterious affliction that causes all the seedlings in your flats to suddenly fall over and die when they were perfectly healthy the night before.

It is caused by fungus. The best way of protecting seedlings from this devastating disease is to start the seeds in sterile soil mix and be careful not to overwater.

DRAINAGE Refers to the ease with which water removes itself from the soil. In clay soil the drainage tends to be poor and too slow; in sandy soil it tends to be too good and too fast. Humusy, loamy soil holds water long enough for plant roots to take it up but not so long that they sit in water beyond the point where they can use it. Very important in container and house-plant gardening, as well as in the open garden.

DRIP LINE Where water falls on the ground when it drips off the leaves. That's the place fertilizer should be added once the leaves are mature, because the plant's surface roots have reached the drip line at that point in their growth and, therefore, fertilizer placed there will be most quickly taken up by the plant. (This applies, of course, to surface roots, not to the deeper roots.)

See also Side Dressing.

FERTILIZER What the plant eats from. Unless you have a great deal of rich compost to incorporate in the soil, you will have to add some fertilizer regularly in order to grow a good crop of vegetables.

There are two kinds of fertilizers: organic and inorganic. (*See* Chemical Fertilizers.) If you want a bumper crop, better nutrition, and a healthier world for yourself and future generations, use only organic fertilizer.

Organic fertilizers are not man-made; they are natural products—anything you would find in nature, from plants to minerals—and they enrich the soil instead of depleting it.

Organic fertilizer encourages the growth of soil bacteria, which break down the plant nutrients into a form the plant can use. It also encourages the growth of earthworms, which perform a number of useful chores in the garden.

Commercial farmers have shown that organic farming is economically feasible and results in increased production. Recent studies have also shown that organically grown vegetables contain more nutrients than those grown inorganically. (*See* chart for Sources of Organic Fertilizers.)

FROST What happens when the temperature of the ground or of plants just above the ground (such as grass) falls from warmer temperatures to that of freezing (32°F.) or lower.

A *light frost* kills only the most delicate plants; a *hard frost* kills everything but the truly winter-hardy plants. Many vegetables—for example, parsnips—taste better after a light frost.

Observation will show you that frost can strike one part of your property and not another. If you have a short growing season, try to site your garden where frost strikes last.

GERMINATION What takes place when seed begins to grow. Different vegetables have different germination rates; that is, take different lengths of time to germinate. Radishes germinate very quickly; parsley is notoriously slow. If you keep a garden journal with planting dates noted, you won't disturb the soil in a flat too soon thinking your parsley has failed to germinate when it has been only ten days since you planted the seeds.

GRANITE DUST An excellent organic source of potassium or potash.

GREENSAND An excellent organic source of potassium or potash.

GYPSUM A soil conditioner; adds some calcium. Sometimes used to reduce soil acidity.

HARDENING-OFF The process of gradually introducing plants to outdoor conditions. Plants started indoors should not be placed outside abruptly; they need time to adapt. This can be accomplished by putting them in a cold frame, or by gradually allowing them to adjust to the outdoors. Take them outside during the day (but not if it is very windy) for about two weeks. Be sure to bring them inside for the night. By the end of this time, they should be sufficiently acclimatized to adjust well to the naturally changing day and night temperatures.

In actual practice, I rarely have the patience to do this for two full weeks. Use your judgment (and the weather forecast) if you want to take a chance and set them in the ground sooner. If a cold spell creeps up on you, you can always protect the plants with paper bags.

Some plants, like lettuce, prefer cooler weather and, at a certain point, will be so much happier outdoors that they won't even mind fairly cold weather. Warmth-loving plants, like eggplants and tomatoes, will die if set out too soon and too suddenly.

HEAVY FROST *See* Frost.

HEAVY SOIL *See* Clay Soil.

HEEL IN To protect plants when you don't have time to plant them right away. When you order plants from a seedhouse, you can't always plant them as soon as you get them. Water them well; then, temporarily, heel them in. This should be done as follows: dig a shallow trench with one side at an acute angle. Set the plants against the sloping side of the trench and cover the roots; leave the tops above the soil but resting against the side of the trench. Don't leave them this way too long before permanently planting them.

HILL A circular flat saucerlike depression. No one knows why this is called a hill, but it seems it always has been. Needless to say, this definition applies only to gardening practice, as "Plant zucchini and cucumbers in hills." Webster's defines it as "Several seeds or plants planted in a group rather than a row." This is true, but it should also say in a circular depression, because part of the function of the "hill" is to retain water a little longer than a flat area would.

Not to be confused with *"hilling,"* which means to draw the earth up around the plant.

HOTBED A heated cold frame.

HUMUS Compost when it is completely decomposed. It is dark and smells like the woods after a rain. The texture is even and pleasantly crumbly.

A loamy soil (the most desirable kind) is rich in humus, and the best thing you can ever say about a soil is that it is "humusy." Humus conditions soil, adds nutrients, and is good in every way.

Unfortunately, not all dark or "black" soil is humus, and even humus, when old, may have had all the nutrients leached out of it (as in old peat areas).

Some forms of peat commercially available have been

decomposed almost to the point of humus; this is good to add to your garden if you can afford it.

INORGANIC GARDENING Gardening with chemicals instead of with natural substances. *See* Fertilizer and Insecticides.

INSECTICIDES Substances that kill insects. DDT is an insecticide—which tells you immediately that some insecticides aren't good for people, either.

Insecticides are indiscriminate killers; they destroy good insects as well as the ones you want to get rid of. Ideally, it would be best to use no insecticides at all. If you feel you must, at least limit yourself to pyrethrum and other organically acceptable insecticides; above all, avoid the inorganically acceptable ones that pollute the air and earth, and are harmful to man and beast as well as to good insects.

Unfortunately, the Department of Agriculture is not a good guide to insecticides; it recommends many that no responsible organic gardener would use. *Organic Gardening* magazine prints many, many suggestions for avoiding the use of insecticides completely. Try companion planting of such things as garlic and onions among your other vegetables to repel aphids; marigolds to repel hornworms and whitefly, and to attract slugs, which can then be easily collected in a can of salted water; and parsley to attract the celery worm and keep it off your celery. I have found companion planting fun and practical. It's pretty, too: rows of marigolds in front of the tomatoes, eggplants, and other vegetables.

Some organic gardeners make a spray of cayenne pepper, garlic, and onion and use it freely. I haven't ever tried it but it certainly wouldn't hurt.

INTERCROPPING The technique of growing a crop that matures quickly in closer than normal proximity to one that matures slowly. For instance, plant radishes and beets in front of tomatoes. Intercropping gives maximum yield for the amount of space available and is highly recommended.

KELP A common brown seaweed found along the coastal areas. It is a wonderful fertilizer, rich in potash, nitrogen, and other minerals. Collect it when you're at the beach and scatter it around your garden to be dug in next time you rototill.

LEACHING The draining of nutrients out of the soil through the percolation of water. Good soil requires good drainage, but each drop of water carries some food away with it. If you have an exceptionally wet season, fertilize more than usual to counteract this leaching effect.

LEGGY The appearance of seedlings when you grow them indoors without enough light. They get tall and spindly instead of sturdy and compact. Strangely enough, this will also happen if your starting soil mix is too rich. Pinching them back helps some, but it is best not to let it happen in the first place.

LIGHT FROST *See* Frost.

LIME Ground limestone is the least expensive and best alkaline substance you can use to counteract soil acidity; it also conditions the soil. Do not use quicklime by mistake; it is quite different and harmful to the plants.

Most gardens need to be limed at least every three years; only a soil test can tell for sure.

Wood ashes are a good source of lime, and rich in potassium, too. They can be used much more freely than limestone, and, if scattered on the surface, provide protection against slugs until the next rain.

MANURE A soil conditioner as well as a fertilizer. Use it generously no matter what else you put in your garden.

If you can get fresh manure, put it aside and do not use until it is well rotted. Commercial manures—bagged, nicely dried, and practically deodorized—are available. Some gardeners feel that commercial manure is so overprocessed that it is practically worthless, but the fresh is sometimes difficult to store. I have to rely on the commercial manure and can only hope they aren't ruining it completely.

Manure varies considerably, depending upon the animal it comes from. Horse manure is considered the most desirable for all-around use, although rabbit manure has recently come to be held in high esteem. Both rabbit and chicken manure are high in nitrogen, and this should be kept in mind when applying them.

MATURITY DATE The number of days it will take a seed to become a ripe cucumber, carrot, or whatever the crop is. Most home gardeners pick vegetables long before that time, since tender, immature vegetables are one of the delights of home gardening.

It is, however, a good guide in planning your garden, and will tell you whether your growing season is long enough to include a certain vegetable.

With vegetables that are normally started indoors, the number of days to maturity indicated in the seed catalog starts from the day the plant is set out in the open garden, *not from the day the seed is sown.*

MULCH Organic material applied on top of the soil in the garden. It can be hay, grass clippings, buckwheat hulls, straw, or even leaves (although these should be shredded so they will not form a soggy, matted mass) . Mulching is good garden practice and will save you hours of cultivating, watering, and weeding; the mulch will eventually decompose and enrich the soil. Do not let mulch touch the stems of plants or it will rot them.

NITROGEN One of the "big three" fertilizers. The first fertilizer listed in formulas, such as 5–10–10. Essential to leafy growth and general health of all plants.

Bone meal, cottonseed meal, and rabbit and poultry manure are all good sources of organic nitrogen.

ORGANIC FERTILIZERS *See* Fertilizer.

ORGANIC GARDENING Gardening the natural way, without the use of man-made fertilizers or insecticides. By far the best for the environment and for you. Once you have tried gardening organically, you will never want to do it any other way; food tastes better and is better for you; crops are more productive. If you do it with your own compost heap and with generous use of mulch, it is undoubtedly the least expensive and most work-free way to garden.

PEAT POTS Containers made of compressed peat. They come rectangular and round, and in several sizes. Their great advantage over clay pots is that the plant can be set out in the open garden without removing it from the peat pot, which will, theoretically, disintegrate into the soil. Transplants grown in clay or plastic pots must be taken out of the pots, and this inevitably disturbs the root system and sets back the growth of the plant.

Tip. Peat pots don't always disintegrate as they are supposed to. Be sure to bury the pot completely; do not let the rim protrude above the level of the soil or it will not disintegrate. At least an hour before planting, wet the pot thoroughly by soaking it in water, and make a few slashes in the sides with a sharp knife to help the roots push through.

PESTICIDES Chemicals that kill garden pests, such as insects, fungi, slugs. They also kill beneficial insects, such as bees and ladybugs. There are many alternatives to pesticides that should be used. If you use any, be sure they are approved by organic gardeners.

PESTS AND DISEASES Animals, insects, and fungi that damage plants and interfere with the crop. Your own dog or cat falls into that category when he digs up the neighbors' petunias.

Animals. Fencing is the only sure way of coping with rabbits, cats, woodchucks, and deer. Occasionally you will get a woodchuck that will climb a fence; a loose wire strung around the top will usually deter even him. Squirrels are a special problem and can get into any garden that isn't caged (that is, a fence roof as well as four fence walls), but most of the time squirrels won't bother anything but corn.

Insects. Mulching, black plastic, wood ashes, dust of various herbs and spices (cayenne, garlic, black pepper), and companion planting of marigolds, garlic, onions, and some other flowers and herbs will sometimes deter harmful insects. Often the damage they do to healthy plants is minimal and not worth the panic button some gardeners push the minute they see a white butterfly hovering over their broccoli. Hand-picking solves a lot of problems; lightly salted water will take care of most of the ills of the cabbage family. Spraying your vegetables regularly with a fairly hard stream of water from the hose will deter aphids and whitefly—so will companion planting of marigolds, which also deter nematodes and are attractive to slugs. (The slugs will eat the marigolds instead of the eggplants.)

Diseases. Unless the disease seems to be spreading unduly, do not let it worry you. A little leaf miner won't eat anywhere near as much of your Swiss chard as you will, and the more pernicious diseases will take over in spite of anything you can do. Remove the damaged leaves if there are only a few of them—this method works especially well to curb leaf miner.

Most of the time you will still get a good crop even if your tomatoes, for instance, seem to be withering away; just make a note to check with your county agent on what disease it is, and plant a resistant variety in a different spot next year.

Tip. Prevention is better than attempted cure. Keep the weeds down in and around your garden; mulch, fertilize, and water on schedule—do everything you can to make your plants healthy and sturdy enough to fend for themselves.

pH Also known as soil reaction. The pH scale is a method of measuring the acidity/alkalinity factor of the soil. The scale runs from 1 to 14, with 7.0 indicating completely neutral (neither acid nor alkaline) ; below 7.0 is acid, above 7.0 is alkaline.

Most vegetables will do perfectly well in a range of 6.0 to 7.0. Only a soil test can tell you what your soil is. *See* Soil Test.

PHOSPHATE ROCK Also called rock phosphate. Excellent source of phosphorus.

Available inorganically as superphosphate, which is rock phosphate that has been treated with sulfuric acid; not recommended for organic gardening. Pure rock phosphate is what you want.

PHOSPHORUS Another of the "big three" fertilizers, listed second in formulas such as 5–10–10. Essential for all vegetables and especially important for root vegetables.

PINCHING BACK To "pinch" or nip off the tips of plants with scissors or the nails of your thumb and forefinger.

Pinching back is done to make plants bushier, to make

them grow laterally (as in the case of cucumbers) , or to increase the size of their fruit.

POTASH *See* Potassium.

POTASSIUM The third listed of the "big three" elements in formulas such as 5–10–10. Makes plants winter hardy as well as sturdier in general. Wood ashes are a good source; also granite dust and greensand.

PYRETHRUM A natural insecticide that even our grandparents knew about. It is made from chrysanthemums and is used as a spray or dust. It does not harm plants or people.

ROTOTILLING A mechanical way to spade up your garden. You can hire someone to do it for you or buy your own machine. I have it done in the spring as soon as the ground has dried out enough to be worked. Before the actual rototilling, I spread fertilizer and manure so that it is dug in.

Rototilling is a great work-saver, although the home-garden-size machine goes about only six inches deep and leaves many large rocks just below that depth. If you are starting a new garden, spade over afterward with a fork spade to get all the large rocks and do an extra-good job.

Rototilling should be done in the spring, sufficiently in advance of planting to allow fertilizers and conditioners to settle in and start to work in the soil. However, some gardeners also rototill in the fall, to allow winter frosts to kill pests and bacteria and to break up the clods. If you have the time and the expense is no problem, it could be done both spring and fall to good effect.

Tip. If you use mulch, have it dug in instead of removing it; it will mean going over with the rototiller more times, but the results are well worth it.

SALT HAY Hay gathered from salt marshes along the shore. Excellent for mulch. Don't worry about the salt; it isn't enough to hurt the garden in any way.

SEAWEED We've come full circle on this one. Our great-grandparents knew that seaweed and fishheads were great fertilizers; somewhere along the way we forgot. Now there has been a rediscovery of seaweed as fertilizer and, along with fish emulsions, it is available from organic gardening centers as well as along the shore. *See also* Kelp.

SEEDLING A young plant—from the first two leaves it sends up from seed to the early growth it makes after transplanting.

SET To begin to form fruit. Sometimes flowers, the forerunners of the fruit, drop off without "setting." This can be due to a number of things, such as the fact that the first flowers are often male and don't ever produce fruit, or that weather conditions are unfavorable—tomatoes, for instance, will not set unless the weather is warm enough (but not too hot). Not usually a serious problem.

Tip. If you don't seem to have enough bees for good pollination, plant bee balm or borage outside the garden to attract them. I never plant them in the garden, because I don't have the room and because I prefer not to garden in the midst of *quite* that many bees.

If lack of bees isn't your problem and your tomatoes are still not setting, try a preparation like Blossom Set or gently shake your plants to help them self-pollinate. (This won't work with eggplants or zucchini or most other plants, but setting is not often a problem with them.)

SIDE DRESSING Laying a bead of fertilizer alongside a row of plants. *See* Drip Line.

SOIL The earth's surface covering. The top two layers are top-soil and subsoil. Plants grow primarily in the first layer, the fertile topsoil. We are gradually depleting our topsoil, so that many areas where it used to be 20 inches deep are now only 12 inches or even less. The average vegetable gardener is lucky if he has four to six inches.

Good soil management eventually deepens the layer of topsoil; poor soil management and reliance on chemical fertilizers deplete it.

Subsoil is the comparatively infertile layer below topsoil. If you dig a trench with straight sides, you can usually recognize the point where topsoil and subsoil meet; subsoil is lighter in color and of a different consistency.

Tip. In spading, don't ever put the light-colored subsoil over your topsoil. Also, beware of builders who bury your topsoil under subsoil or, worse yet, sell your topsoil and leave you a new house surrounded by subsoil. If this should happen, you won't be able to grow a lawn or anything else unless you bring in yards of topsoil.

SOIL BACTERIA These are the workers in the factory that is good humusy soil; they convert the nutrients into a form the plant roots can utilize. Without soil bacteria, all the organic material in the world will not feed your vegetables. Inorganic chemical fertilizers destroy soil bacteria; organic fertilizers help them to multiply, and they in turn increase the fertility and condition of the soil.

Topsoil is formed partly by the action of soil bacteria. If future generations are to have anything but sterile soil in which to grow their flowers, trees, and vegetables, we must encourage the flourishing of these indispensable soil bacteria.

SOIL COMPACTION This is what happens to soil if you walk on it when it is wet, and it is why you should be especially careful to keep off your lawn in winter and early spring. A heavy weight (even a child) will compact or press together the soil particles so that plant roots cannot penetrate as easily as they should. It is a difficult condition to correct.

Tip. Once you have rototilled your garden, keep to the aisles as much as possible or you will undo all the good of rototilling.

SOIL DEFICIENCY The lack of sufficient quantity of an essential ingredient (nitrogen or boron, for example) in the soil. Some deficiencies are more serious than others in their effect on crop yield, but for best results all should be available in a natural balance.

The appearance of your plants will usually give you a clue to any serious deficiency. Even trace elements, in spite of the minute quantities in which they occur, will affect plant growth and health if they are insufficient.

The best way to keep a good level of essential elements in the soil is with compost, peat moss, manure, and organic fertilizers. These provide soil bacteria with fuel for their "food factories."

Chemical fertilizers quickly leach out of the soil, are not worked on by soil bacteria, and need to be replenished constantly. They do not furnish the fringe benefits of trace elements (as do organic fertilizers) .

SOIL TEST An analysis of certain components of the soil to determine whether or not they are present in sufficient quantity. In addition, it rates for alkalinity/acidity. A soil test will determine how much nitrogen, phosphorus, and potassium you need to apply, as well as how much lime or peat moss; recommendations on trace minerals may also be given.

You can do soil testing yourself with a special kit available from any garden center, or send soil samples to your nearest Extension Center, which will do it for you free.

Tip. If you have several gardens, get a soil test done for each one; they can vary considerably.

STAKING Tying a plant to a support so that it won't fall over or grow along the ground. Tomatoes can be staked or not, as you please, but eggplants, as well as some other plants, should always be staked.

There are various methods of staking: by tying to a fence, by putting stakes in the ground next to the plant, or by putting a cage or support around the plant.

Put in stakes when setting out the plant. If you wait to do it until the plants need staking, there is danger of damaging the roots in the process of driving in the stakes.

Don't use wire for tying; use a soft string or the covered Twist 'Ems and tie loosely, leaving room for stem growth.

Tip. To make more efficient use of garden space, grow plants like cucumbers, melons, and vegetable spaghetti on a fence; the crop will be larger, less prone to disease, and easier to harvest.

SUN SCALD What sometimes happens to tomatoes if exposed to too much direct sun. (Usually their foliage is a natural protection against this problem.) The tomatoes turn a dull tan color and the skin gets tough—not very good eating.

THINNING Some seeds are so small that you cannot sow them the proper distance apart; some, like beets, which are three seeds in one, will need thinning even when planted exactly the right distance for the mature plant. Since you won't get strong healthy plants if they grow all crowded together, you need to remove some in order to give the others room to grow. This process is called "thinning."

Do not attempt to thin until the seedlings are tall enough and far enough along so that you can see which are healthy and which look weak. Take out the weak ones and leave the sturdier plants, wherever possible. (Sometimes this will mean a little transplanting when two sturdy plants are growing close together.)

Many vegetables—beets, lettuce, Swiss chard—can be left until the thinnings are large enough to eat.

Tip. The usual method of thinning is to pull up the plants being thinned; a better way is to cut them off at ground level with a small, sharp scissors. With this method you don't disturb the roots of the plants that are left. It may mean doing it again to one or two plants, but it is well worth the little extra trouble.

TRACE ELEMENTS Nutrients normally available in the soil in very small quantities, as contrasted with nitrogen or phosphorus, for example. In spite of the minute "traces" in which they occur, agriculturists have become increasingly aware that these nutrients are important; lack of them seriously affects crops.

Among the trace elements are boron, cobalt, copper, iron, manganese, molybdenum, and zinc. (*See* chart for Sources of Organic Fertilizer.)

In addition to the importance of trace elements to plant health, nutritionists and specialists in body chemistry have discovered that these same elements are important to healthy human growth; lack of zinc, for example, is thought to contribute to shortness of stature. It would seem only reasonable to assume that vegetables grown in soils with adequate trace-elements content would be better as human food than plants grown in deficient soils. To be sure of adequate trace elements, use organic fertilizers and compost.

TRANSPLANTING For various reasons, not all plants are started where they are to grow. Moving them from their original seedbed to their final growing site is "transplanting."

The single most important rule in transplanting is to make sure the soil is carefully firmed around the roots the entire depth of the root structure and beneath it; air pockets left in the soil can kill the whole plant.

Always water well and mist frequently the first week of transplanting, even if you used peat pots. *See* Peat Pots.

Some transplants should be set at the same level in which they have been growing; some should be set much deeper. See instructions for culture of individual vegetables.

TRUE LEAVES The first two leaves a seedling puts forth are not "true leaves." The second pair are, and can be recognized by their shape, characteristic of the mature plant.

Seedlings should not under any circumstances be fertilized or transplanted until the true leaves appear; there are sufficient nutrients in the seed to sustain growth up to that point.

VERMICULITE A kind of mica, finely ground; it is an excellent sterile starting medium for seedlings. Mixed with soil and peat moss, it is good for house plants.

VIABLE A seed that is still alive and capable of germinating is viable. How long a seed will stay viable varies according to the vegetable.

If you are in doubt about the viability of your seed, put a few between two moistened sheets of paper toweling. Keep the toweling moist for as long as the seed normally takes to germinate; the temperature should be between 70 and 85 degrees. If the seeds sprout, they are still viable and can be planted normally. Since some seeds stay viable five years or longer, it is always worth checking them out.

WET FEET An expression used to describe the condition where water stays in the soil or the saucer of a potted plant so that the plant roots are kept constantly wet. Watercress likes wet feet; sweet potatoes hate it. Not to be confused with keeping the soil *moist*.

WINTER HARDY Plants that are described as winter hardy can safely be left in the open garden over the winter; many root crops fall into this category. If the plant in question is a shrub, it may be winter hardy and still suffer some damage over the winter. The branches that are dead in the spring are said to have suffered from "winterkill." A little of this is normal; remove them from the bush, which will then be perfectly healthy.

CHAPTER THREE

How to Grow Tomatoes

TOMATOES ARE BY FAR the most popular of all the vegetables grown in the home garden; they are also very easy to grow. I once knew a commercial photographer who spent long summer hours in his large, loftlike studio in the heart of the city of Stamford, Connecticut. In the still hard-packed, weed-filled earth along the sunny front wall leading to the entrance to his studio, he grew large, unbelievably healthy tomato plants. After a sometimes tense morning's work, he would relax by watering and talking to his plants; in August, he was picking fresh tomatoes for lunch. If tomatoes would grow there, they will grow almost anywhere.

Considerable impetus has been given to home-grown tomatoes by the decline of the quality of store-bought ones. The *New York Times* food editors are practically rabid on the subject of the tasteless objects available commercially, and, judging from reader response, many consumers agree with them whole-heartedly. I almost never buy a "fresh" tomato; I don't think they are worth eating until I can pick them from my garden. Out of season, I think, canned tomatoes taste better and fresher than the strange store tomatoes that have been picked green, ripened by gas, and packed in pallid packets under cellophane.

Ruth Stout suggests freezing your crop for out-of-season use. She says you can freeze them whole, then thaw and eat them like fresh tomatoes. I have never had success with this method; mine always thaw out mushy and watery.

Seedsmen have responded to the widespread interest in tomatoes by developing many new varieties and disease-resistant hybrids; most are variations of the standard round red tomato. Something seems to have happened to the tremendous variety of tomatoes I remember from childhood. The farmer next door grew many, many different kinds—all shapes, sizes, and shades of red, pink, and yellow—for his blue-ribbon exhibits at the Danbury Fair. I grew up taking his varied harvest much for granted, but you hardly ever see them any more.

Another tomato that has lost ground in modern times is the beefsteak. Although not perfectly shaped or smooth, rather ungainly, with a tendency to crack, the beefsteak has a flavor and meaty texture unsurpassed by any other tomato—and one slice covers a whole piece of bread for a sandwich. When you buy tomato plants, you will often hear old-time gardeners asking whether there are any beefsteaks.

History

Tomatoes are a native American vegetable, but they were not known to the early colonists. They originated in South America, where they still grow wild. Artifacts show tomatoes were cultivated by the Aztecs as long ago as two thousand years. The Indians spread them from the Andes up through Central America to Mexico; for some reason they never caught on with North American Indians.

It will come as no surprise that the Italians were the first Europeans to appreciate and make use of this exotic New World fruit. While other Europeans still considered the tomato just another poisonous nightshade plant, suitable only for ornamental gardens, Italians were cooking it in delicious dishes as early as the sixteenth century. They called it *pomo Peruviano* and *pomo d'oro,* which would seem to indicate that the first tomatoes came to Europe from Peru and were yellow rather than red.

By the eighteenth century, the tomato was grown for eating throughout Europe, England, and America, and was included by Jefferson in his kitchen garden. The French became so fond of it they named it *pomme d'amour,* or love apple, and attributed aphrodisiac qualities to it.

One of the features that slowed the acceptance of tomato as a food is the strong, slightly unpleasant odor of the foliage; early gardeners thought that anything that smelled like that must be unhealthy.

Types: Determinate and Indeterminate

Before you plant tomatoes, you should know there are two distinct types; determinate and indeterminate.

Most of the varieties found in the average home garden are indeterminate; they keep growing at the tip unless pinched back, and will continue to set fruit until frost kills the plant. An indeterminate plant can grow to a tremendous height (or length, if you haven't staked it) ; fifteen feet is not unusual.

Determinate types will stop growing when they reach a certain height, set and ripen fruit all at the same time, then cease producing. This is a distinct plus if you want to process your tomato crop; most paste tomatoes (the best kind for processing) are determinate. Determinate types will also produce an earlier crop than most indeterminate types.

When to Plant

Since tomatoes are sensitive to cold, they must be grown from seed indoors. You can do this yourself quite easily, or you can buy plants from a local nursery when it is time to set them in the open garden.

If you start your own seedlings, do so five to eight weeks before the last frost date in your area.

How to Plant

Tomato seeds are considered hard to germinate. The seed is fine and should be planted 1/2 inch deep in sterilized soil mix in peat pots. When ready to set out, stand the transplants 18"–36" apart (depending on the variety and whether you are staking them). Rows should be 36"–60" apart. I never grow tomatoes in rows, because I always grow them along a fence. However you grow them, leave enough room between plants for good air circulation; it will cut down on disease.

To set out transplants, harden off (*see* Glossary, page 23) and dig holes deep enough to put a cup of good 10–10–10 fertilizer and a cup of manure in the bottom—at least 6 inches below the root of the transplant. Fill in the next 3 inches with earth mixed with a cup of the same mixture. Top off with plain soil. Remove the bottom two to four leaves (more if the plant has become leggy), and plant up to three-quarters of the stem in the earth. The stem will send out roots and will give you sturdier, healthier plants.

In setting out transplants, protect them from cutworms by wrapping a 2-inch-wide collar of foil loosely around the stem; an inch should extend below the soil, an inch above it.

Always water transplants copiously when setting them out and for the next week or so until they have taken hold. They are not easily set back by transplanting, but they do need sufficient moisture to encourage the roots to form and reach out into new soil.

Culture

Tomatoes need a full eight hours of sun. This means from the time they germinate; if you are growing seedlings indoors, provide adequate light to take the place of the sun. As plants grow, the light will have to be raised. A fixed light source will not be satisfactory; it will either be too far away in the beginning or the growing plants will bump into it. Lights must be on pulleys, raised and lowered as conditions warrant.

If your seedlings start to get leggy and spindly, chances are they are not getting enough light.

Do not overfeed seedlings; they will get too large to handle properly and will force you to set them out in the open garden too soon. If they do get too big, transfer them to larger pots. *With the right care and conditions, you can even bring them to the point of setting fruit indoors;* a much earlier crop will result. However, this takes careful management and a lot of indoor room.

Tip. Keep tomato seedlings away from your regular house plants; they may pick up whitefly from an infested plant.

It is more practical to start seeds indoors in peat pots than in a flat. However, many gardeners feel that peat pots can be a problem; they sometimes prevent the roots from breaking through the pot. To avoid this contingency, *soak the pots in water an hour or so before planting*—you might even make slashes in the sides with a sharp knife to help the roots push through the pot once it is in the ground.

Tomatoes need a great deal of moisture, and it must be provided on a regular schedule, not erratically. Alternate dry and moist conditions, or excessively moist conditions, may result in blossom-end rot.

When plants begin to flower, fertilize with a cup of manure and a half cup of 10–10–10. Scratch lightly into surface of the soil so as not to disturb the feeder roots, and water in a little.

Staking—or Not

To stake or not to stake, that is the question. It depends partly on room; unstaked plants sprawl over a wide area and take up much more room than staked plants. Staking keeps fruit from rotting on wet ground and protects the plant, to some extent, from insects and diseases. I can't see any good reason not to stake. The work isn't all that hard—just set in 7'–8' 2″ x 2″ poles next to the plant at the same time that you transplant it to the open garden. As the plant grows, tie it up to the stake for support—especially before a thunder shower when the hard rain may otherwise beat it to the ground. Use soft cord or Twist 'Ems, twice around the stake and once, loosely, around the stem.

When you get your 8-foot stakes up next to your transplants, they will seem all out of proportion. The first year I raised my tomatoes organically and went to 8-foot stakes, my neighbor came over and eyed the result with raised eyebrows. "What are you building—a garage?" he teased. I showed him the tomato plants two months later. The stakes were buried out of sight in foliage, and I had had to guy-wire them to short stakes set into the ground outside the fence. The plants had grown over the fence and down to the hay I had put on the ground on the other side. Sometimes when I tell this story, someone says knowingly, "All foliage and no fruit, eh?" But as any organic gardener would guess, the vines were heavy with tomatoes and the fruit and foliage very much in proportion.

If you don't stake, it is especially important to mulch with straw or hay so that the fruit doesn't rest on bare earth.

Other Ways of Supporting Tomatoes

Unless you are letting them sprawl, most tomatoes, even those grown in containers, need some kind of support if they are a variety that reaches more than a couple of feet in height. As container gardening has become more popular, a number of interesting ways of supporting tomatoes have been developed. They all work very well; it's simply a matter of time and personal preference. Staking is the simplest. Another method, which works equally well in the ground or in containers, is *caging.*

Caging is done by setting fencing in a circle around the plant. Be sure the circle is large enough to accommodate the mature plant. The tomatoes will grow up inside the cage and the plant won't have to be staked for support.

The only disadvantage to this method is getting your hand through the cage to pick ripe tomatoes; with beefsteaks, it's also a problem to get the tomato back through the holes. Use chicken wire rather than regular garden fencing; it's not so strong but the holes are larger.

Ordinary rose trellises make attractive tomato-plant supports. Tie the plant to the trellis as it grows. You may want to prune the suckers and some of the growth to conform somewhat to the shape of the trellis; otherwise the plant may get too wide and stick out far from its support. A tomato plant that has to be pulled in too far to be tied to its support looks as uncomfortable as a fat lady cinching her waist too much to create an illusion of slimness.

The most interesting way of supporting tomato plants is the

newest and the most work; that is to *espalier* them. Here you must train the plant, just as you do fruit trees, to conform rigidly to the shape of your espalier. It means judicious pruning and constant care; tomatoes don't grow as neatly as apple trees. I have never had the patience to do this, although I admire the result; you certainly wouldn't want to do it with more than one or two plants. I don't know, either, how you would deal with the problem of sun scald, since there would obviously be a great deal of fruit with comparatively little foliage. But a board-and-batten garage wall with a neatly espaliered tomato plant loaded with scarlet fruit would certainly be a beautiful sight.

An easy way to grow the smaller, so-called container tomatoes is in *hanging baskets*. I have indicated, under varieties, some that are good for this type of gardening. They make very decorative hanging plants, grow enormous clusters of cherry-sized fruit, and are easy to care for if you are careful to give them enough fertilizer and water. They don't need any support at all.

Suckers

This is a much-debated area of tomato growing. Suckers are shoots that sprout between the main stem and the branches at the point where they meet. They grow profusely in no time and make the plant very bushy.

Until recently, good garden practice recommended removing all suckers soon after the second pair of leaves appeared. Now the tide has turned slightly and advice varies. Some say remove the first several sets of suckers (on lower branches) and let the rest grow two to three inches before pinching back. Others say leave them be. Since I don't have time to do any extra work, I must confess I tended to let the suckers alone the first couple of seasons. Then I tried, one year, pruning all the suckers off some plants and leaving all of them on others. I had far more fruit from the unpruned plants and, after all, a good harvest is what vegetable gardening is all about. Now I have to sort of sidle past the plants because they get very bushy (even staked), but my tomatoes never get sun scald even in the hottest, sunniest weather.

By the way, don't worry that the foliage will get so thick the sun won't be able to get to the tomato to ripen it; the sun does not ripen tomatoes and it may damage them. Tomatoes will ripen nicely even though completely shaded by their foliage; in fact, *in ripening tomatoes in the house, never put them on a sunny windowsill.*

Harvest

A tomato is ripe when you think it is. I had an uncle who always grabbed a salt shaker and headed for the garden as soon as he had pulled into the driveway; he liked to eat green tomatoes and could never persuade anyone to pick them that way for him.

Tomatoes will ripen gradually until suddenly more are ready than you can eat out of hand; plan to do your processing when this peak is reached. Canning, making sauce, freezing, pickling are all ways of making the most of your crop.

Late in the season, watch out for frost forecasts. With luck, you will have a great number of tomatoes still on the vine. Pick all of them. The green tomatoes, in all stages, will make wonderful pickles, relishes, and fried tomatoes. Any with the faintest show of change of color—even from dark green to light green—can be ripened off the vine. Just wrap them individually in newspaper and lay them gently in cartons, layer upon layer. Spot-check regularly; if you have wrapped them in order of their degree of ripeness, you'll find they ripen fairly well on schedule, and you'll have fresh tomatoes on your table for Thanksgiving dinner—or even later.

If you have the room, you can store them directly on wax-paper-lined open shelves in a dark place. The ideal storage temperature for both methods is 65°F.

Varieties

One of the reasons I grow more tomato plants than I should is that after my plan is made, I always come upon just one or two more I can't resist trying. Your choice should depend partly on what you want; if tomatoes are a little acid for your taste, try yellow ones; if pressed for room, try container-gardening varieties; if you want a spectacular salad bar for summer buffets, grow all the fascinating different shapes and colors. Or if your family are big sandwich eaters or brown-baggers, by all means include the beefsteaks.

Unless you have a special reason for doing otherwise, choose among the disease-resistant varieties. Look for the initials V, F, or N. V stands for verticillium resistant; F for fusarium wilt resistant; N for nematode resistant. You will also sometimes see H, which simply means it is a hybrid.

In seed catalogs, tomato varieties are usually listed more or less as follows: "Early," "Main Season," "Late Season," "Orange" (or "Yellow" or "Pink"), "Container," and "Paste." Sometimes two of these groups will be lumped together; thus, "Early and Midseason" might also include "Late" under "Midseason." You will have to search out for yourself which are determinate and indeterminate; catalog listings don't invariably say. They will indicate, however, by such phrases as "will bear up to frost," which obviously means indeterminate.

Although miniature and cherry tomatoes are usually listed as "Container," they are equally good in the open garden. It is just that they have a more compact growth habit and are easily grown in the limited space of containers; also the proportion of fruit to foliage makes them especially decorative. However, remember that all tomatoes were once grown in Europe purely as ornamentals, so if you want full-sized fruit, do not hesitate to grow a standard tomato in a container. Of course, it will have to be a larger container than for a patio type, and you will have either to stake the plant or allow it enough room to spread in its normal fashion.

Any tomato, regardless of variety, can be grown in the ground, in a container, or indoors—always providing you meet its cultural requirements. Greenhouse-forcing tomatoes *must,* of course, be grown in a greenhouse; it would be too hard to take care of them properly in an apartment—but this is the one exception and the variety is not offered in most catalogs.

If you don't want to spend a lot of time over your choices, you won't go wrong with BIG BOY, BETTER BOY, RAMAPO, FANTAS-TIC, or any of the other popular varieties commonly offered as plants by local nurseries. They are available because they have proved satisfactory.

If you enjoy studying the catalogs and growing unusual varieties, set aside a couple of days for selecting seeds for just this one vegetable. *Stokes lists over eighty varieties, and they do not even begin to include all the ones found in other good catalogs.* Each grower has his own specialties and you can try a few new ones each season along with the ones you have found to work in your garden. You will never get to try them all, because new ones are constantly being developed. Come to think of it, this could be a great hobby—inexpensive and with an unlimited supply of things to collect.

I should warn you that I avoid suggesting any variety developed for commercial markets, even though some of them are supposed to be fairly tasty. It just seems to me that the qualities that make them desirable for picking green, shipping by rail and truck, ripening with gas, handling, lying around the supermarket, or processing by various means are bound to have sacrificed some of the things I like best in a tomato. I lean to any variety which a catalog describes as "good for the home garden"; that means it isn't up to tough commercial standards and is too delicate for shipping—that's for me. No experience I have ever had with a store-bought tomato predisposes me to waste time growing it.

SOME SUGGESTED VARIETIES

Early (Determinate)

SPRINGSET. HVF.

SPRING GIANT. HVF

COLDSET. As its name implies, it will germinate and set fruit in cold weather. (Most tomato seeds won't.) It will also thrive if you happen to have a cold June. For seeding outdoors early, or in areas prone to chilly Junes, this is worth a try.

JETFIRE.

STARFIRE.

NEW YORKER. V.

EARLY GIRL. H. My EARLY GIRL tomatoes gave me mature fruit just one week earlier than my standard tomatoes, so I have never bothered with this variety since. You might have better luck; grow some and see how it works for you.

Main Season and Late: Red (Indeterminate)

MORETON HYBRID.

FANTASTIC. H.

JETSTAR. HVF.

BETTER BOY. HVFN.

CARDINAL. H.

BEEFSTEAK.

GLAMOUR.

BEEFEATER. Also called ITALIAN BEEFSTEAK.

SUPERSONIC. HVF.

BIG GIRL. HVF.

BEEFMASTER. VFN. Beefeater-type.

RAMAPO. HVF.

Main Season and Late: Yellow, Orange, Pink (Indeterminate)

CARO. Red-orange.

JUBILEE. Orange. 2½″–3½″ fruit.

SUNRAY. Orange.

GOLDEN BOY. H.

OXHEART "GIANTISSIMO." Large pink, up to 2½ lbs. each.

YELLOW PLUM. 2″ long, ½″ across.

YELLOW PEAR. 1¾″ × 1″ diam.

RED PEAR.

PONDEROSA. Pink beefsteak-type.

ORANGE QUEEN. Orange beefsteak-type.

KURIHARA. Large pink. A Japanese type offered only by Nichols, so far as I know.

White

The only white variety I have ever heard of is listed in Field's catalog and is named SNOWBALL. Field's describes it as "flesh almost white." If you like novelties, you won't be able to resist this one, but I can't report on it; I have never grown it or known anyone who has. If you do, let me know what you think of it.

Container

Remember, these varieties are not limited to container growing; they are small plants, heavily fruited, very ornamental. If you grow them in the open garden, they self-seed like weeds. Some need to be supported; most do not. The catalog description will guide you.

TINY TIM. 12″–15″ plant. Cherry-sized fruit or slightly larger.
BURPEE PIXIE HYBRID. 18″ plant, 1¾″ fruit.
PRESTO HYBRID. 24″ plant. Fruit the size of a silver dollar.
EARLY SALAD HYBRID. 6″–8″ high, 24″ spread, 1½″ fruit. Good for hanging baskets.
PATIO HYBRID. 30″ plant, 2″ fruit.
SMALL FRY. VF. 3′ or more plant, 1″ fruit. Good for hanging baskets.
PIXIE. 2″ fruit. Thompson & Morgan says: "Sow a few seedlings every month to crop your own tomatoes off your own windowsill every month of the year."
GARDENERS DELIGHT. Fruit the size of a large walnut. Only Thompson & Morgan has this, and they really rave about it. In their flavor chart it is one of the few tomatoes that get a "Supreme" rating.

Paste

If you plan to make tomato paste or sauce, this type of tomato has much more solids and much less juice than the standard variety. The Italian plum tomato is this type. You can, of course, make sauce with the standard tomato, but to do so you will either have to add tomato paste or reduce the liquid considerably; otherwise your sauce will be too watery.

Almost all paste tomatoes are determinate; your crop will mature all at once and then there will be no more fruit. For canning purposes, this is ideal.

Some gardeners like paste tomatoes for salads and eating also; I prefer the standards. However, if you are growing some anyhow, try them raw and make up your own mind.

ROMA. VF.
VERONA. VF.
REX CHICO.
SAN MARZANO.

CHAPTER FOUR

How to Grow Lettuces and Other Greens

THE WORLD OF salad "greens" is much wider than most gardeners and cooks realize. In addition to Belgian endive, all the true cabbages, Chinese cabbage, summer (or New Zealand) spinach, true spinach, chicory, escarole, and watercress, there is the great variety of lettuces: Oak Leaf, Salad Bowl, Ruby, Romaine, Butterhead, and Iceberg, to name only the leading ones. And this list doesn't even touch on the many mustards, lamb's-quarters, dandelions, and myriad other tasty leaves enjoyed all over the world but mostly neglected in the United States.

Doing justice to the entire range of edible greens would take a whole book just for them; since that is not my intent, I have limited myself to those grown and used in this country. I think you will find some new foods among them; I hope you will be encouraged to make room for them in your garden, as well as in your kitchen.

BELGIAN ENDIVE
Cichorium intybus

I am using "endive" to refer only to WITLOOF CHICORY, also known as French or Belgian endive—the pale, cream-colored, cigar-shaped vegetable found nestled in paper in wooden boxes in the more expensive section of your produce department. Its slightly bitter taste is indescribably delightful, and it is highly prized by gourmet cooks. It is commonly called Belgian endive because most of what is available in our markets is flown in from Belgium. It is very easy, as well as a great deal of fun to grow.

Uses

Although primarily used in this country as a particularly elegant salad green, endive is an excellent and very unusual cooked vegetable. At the prices it goes for in the market, you would never want to serve it that generously, but if you grow your own, you will feel free to try out new recipes with it; in that case, by all means try cooking it.

When to Plant

Plant the seeds in the garden in early summer, so the plants will have time to mature but not go to seed.

Actually, if you have had some in your garden the previous year, you may find a good crop coming up by itself. At least that is what happened to me this year. Last year's plants are four times the size of the seeds I planted this spring. I don't know whether they will all go to seed (probably) or make it to fall (unlikely). If they go to seed, I won't have to order any next spring.

How to Plant

Sow seeds thinly and cover with 1/4 inch of fine soil. Since you are harvesting the roots, the soil should be prepared more deeply than for lettuce or other greens. Plenty of good rich compost or humus and deep fertilizing is advisable. The roots grow surprisingly long.

Thinning

Plants should stand about 12 inches apart in rows 18 inches apart. If you want to transplant your thinnings, do it when plants are about 2"–3" high so the roots will not have got too long.

Culture

Belgian endive is grown in two stages. The first stage takes place in the garden where a tall, erect, somewhat coarse-looking plant sends up its dark green leaves while growing a long tan root. The root is what we are interested in, but the plant is allowed to grow until fall so that it can mature.

It grows without any exceptional care. Light fertilizing during the growing season and plenty of water take care of its cultural requirements.

The second stage comes in the fall. The technical term for what you do then is "forcing."

First dig up the roots. Use a fork spade and dig deep before you heave; the roots are long. Cut off most of the tops, leaving about 2 inches above the shoulder of the root itself. This prevents your cutting the important crown buds.

The next step isn't strictly necessary, but for convenience sake it is always done. Trim the roots from the bottom, so they are all about the same length—usually about 8 or 9 inches. Put aside the ones you want to force right away, store the rest in layers of dry sand; a wooden fruit or vegetable box makes a good container. This storage container should be kept where it will stay cold enough to keep the roots from sprouting but not so cold that it will freeze them.

Then get a good, deep, waterproof container. I use the small-size plastic garbage cans. Take the roots you want to force and set them top end up, touching one another, in the bottom of the container. Fill in between the roots with sand until the whole root and crown are completely covered. Water sand until it is thoroughly moist. The roots should not stand in any actual water, but the sand must be as wet as it can be short of that. Now fill up the garbage can or container with sand or vermiculite or perlite. I use the last because it makes a lighter garbage can in case I need to move it. The material you have just added should be DRY. This is very important or you will rot your endive instead of blanching it. The only reason for adding the dry material is to keep light from the endive as it grows from the root; this is very important if you want to produce edible endive. The dry mixture should be approximately 6"–8" deep.

In three to four weeks, you will notice little shoots peeking up through the dry sand. Go to the market and look at the price of Belgian endive. Then come home, take a sharp paring knife, and feel your way down the shoot to its bottom, about 6 inches. Cut off a nice, plump, cream-colored endive and do what you want with it.

You will harvest one endive for each root you plant, so you will have to judge your own needs in order to tell how many to start forcing and how many to keep in cold storage.

If you want to, you can get a second crop from the same roots. The heads won't be as compact but they will have the same delicious flavor. Just leave the roots undisturbed after the first cutting and they will start producing all over again.

Occasionally the bottom sand will dry out. I wanted to water the bottom layer of sand without wetting the top dry layer of perlite and I was in a quandary until I figured out a way. I took the long, thin accessory that came with my vacuum cleaner—the one for cleaning between old-fashioned radiators and other narrow places. I pushed the narrow end down into the sand and poured water down the wide end that fits over the vacuum-cleaner hose. It worked beautifully. Or you can use a piece of pipe or bamboo—anything slender and hollow.

You can grow endive all winter, and brighten up the usual collection of house plants with this unusual newcomer.

Varieties

No problem here—you're not given a choice. All the catalogs list Belgian endive as WITLOOF CHICORY; look under "chicory" in the index, not under "endive." If you look under endive, you will find only the loose curly heads, similar to escarole, which grow like lettuce.

CABBAGE
Brassica oleracea capitata

Cabbage, like so many other vegetables, has now been developed in varieties that lend themselves to the rigors of nationwide shipping. If you would experience the full delicate flavor and texture of cabbage, benefit fully from its high vitamin content, and enjoy its considerable variety, grow cabbage in your own garden, choosing those unsuited to commercial growing. They will lend color and zip to your salads and make the most wonderful slaws you have ever eaten.

History

Cabbage is an ancient vegetable that originated before the time of horticultural records. The Celts of Western Europe, during their repeated forays around the Mediterranean, apparently introduced it to that area about 600 B.C. *Brassica,* the Latin name for members of the cabbage family, comes from the Celtic word for cabbage.

The Romans, in turn, took it to Britain and through parts of Europe. Around 1541, Jacques Cartier, the French explorer, brought it to Canada where it was adopted by colonists and Indians alike.

Uses

All cabbages can be eaten raw as well as cooked. Oddly enough, their flavor is less strong when raw, and raw cabbage adds more roughage and cellulose to the diet than most salad greens. A cabbage salad a day would certainly keep a lot of digestive problems away.

Raw cabbage is generally shredded; its flavor combines deliciously with fruits—apples and pineapples, for instance—as well as with other raw vegetables.

When to Plant

Cabbage should be started in the house or cellar, whichever is cooler, in early spring—or outdoors in flats in the middle of the summer for late-fall use or winter storage. Sow seeds ½ inch deep. It requires much more care in its early stages if you sow it in the open garden instead of starting it in flats.

Plants are generally available locally; if you do not have facilities for starting seed indoors, plant from bought transplants as soon as the ground can be worked in the spring.

You should be warned that growing cabbage from seed requires a great deal of time and patience. Unless you are an especially dedicated gardener, you will be better advised to give that space in your cellar to tomatoes and peppers, and buy the cabbage plants.

How to Plant

Cabbage plants, whether raised from seed or bought, should be set out in the open garden 12″–18″ apart in the spring, 18″–30″ apart for a winter crop. Rows should be 30 inches apart.

Cabbage requires a rich, fertile, well-drained soil and full sun. Since cabbages are beautiful to look at, consider planting some in your flower beds in front of taller plants such as roses, delphiniums, and lupines. Their neat, compact shape makes them excellent bedding plants.

In the vegetable garden, interplant them with radishes, carrots, and other crops that take up little room and will be pulled up and eaten before cabbages have matured. However, since cabbages require a great deal of nitrogen and phosphorus, you will need to feed them specially; this may affect your root vegetables adversely. If you plan to intercrop cabbages with root vegetables, do it in the early days; you can add nitrogen when the cabbage heads begin to form. Root vegetables need a lot of phosphorus, so the extra fertilizer won't bother them.

Culture

The first time I grew cabbages, I was surprised to find they formed on top of moderately long stalks. I had always pictured them nestled firmly right on top of the earth. They are, but that is because you mound up earth around the stalk as soon as the head begins to form. If you wait too long, the cabbage will become top-heavy and break the stalk. I mound up the earth until the head is sitting on the soil, then mulch it with hay close to the stalk. That way, a wet spell won't rot the outside leaves where they touch the ground.

Fertilize every three weeks with a 10–10–5 fertilizer, and keep well watered; cabbages like a lot of moisture. Do not fertilize heavily at any one time; frequent light feedings are better than shot-in-the-arm applications. A sudden spurt in growth that is due to overfeeding might cause the heads to split.

Harvest

Cabbages can be harvested as soon as the heads are firm. However, winter cabbages can be kept in the garden for some time after that and will stand fairly heavy frost. If you want to store them in the garden instead of the root cellar, pull them out of the ground and stack them upside down on hay. Pile twelve inches of hay on top of them. They will last nicely through the winter and can be brought into the house whenever they are on the menu.

Caution

Some cabbages, especially the large-headed fall/winter ones, do take a great deal of room and are not considered suitable for the really small home garden. I always put cabbages in flower beds, because my vegetable garden area is so small. Also, they attract a number of pests. In spite of this, they are one of the most popular vegetables grown in the home garden, so you will probably want to try your hand at them at least once. If space is a problem, choose the smaller-headed varieties. Plant them more closely than recommended—perhaps 12 inches apart, and harvest before they have fully matured.

Varieties

Cabbages come in all shades of green, as well as several shades of red (the color is really closer to purple) . They come smooth, crinkled (savoy) , round, pointed, large, or midget. You should find choosing your seed or plants an absorbing experience.

Most catalogs list all of the following varieties, plus some special ones of their own. Many growers, such as Burpee, have their own improved strain of a popular variety and describe it accordingly. Listings are usually grouped by when they should be planted; i.e., "Early," "Medium," and "Late." This will guide you in planning your harvesting.

SOME SUGGESTED VARIETIES

Early to Medium
> COPENHAGEN MARKET. YR.
> EARLY JERSEY WAKEFIELD. YR.
> EMERALD CROSS.
> GOLDEN ACRE. YR.
> MARION MARKET.
> STONEHEAD.

Late
> DANISH BULLHEAD.
> FLAT DUTCH.

Savoy
> SAVOY KING.
> CHIEFTAIN.

Red Cabbage
> RED ROCK.
> RED ACRE.
> RED DANISH BULLHEAD.

Note: YR indicates yellows resistant. Check with your county agent to see if this is a problem in your area.

In addition, there is a decorative cabbage that Nichols lists as "MINIATURE JAPANESE ORNAMENTAL CABBAGE." It is also listed in the Gurney catalog. This is so beautiful that it stopped pedestrian traffic when it was grown in large containers outside the main entrance to an elegant resort hotel in New York State. The cold weather brings out a breath-taking array of colors; it would be a conversation piece in the salad bowl of any buffet. It should be planted in late July and would make a nice change of pace for your container gardens. Grow it on a patio, breeze-way, or at your front door for an original and beautiful variation on the eternal pot of geraniums.

If you are really into cabbages, Stokes has an unusually large listing of varieties. Burpee has good color pictures that give you an idea of what the mature cabbage will look like. Burrell has a helpful illustration showing the difference in size and shape of some of the more popular varieties. Thompson & Morgan has a Harvest Guide chart, which rates the flavor and tells the shape of the head and days to harvest for many varieties. All in all, you can easily wile away a couple of dreary winter afternoons planning your cabbage-seed order.

CHICORY AND ESCAROLE
Cichorium endivia

Here we run into a real problem with nomenclature. Technically, these are both endives: chicory is very frilly and curly; escarole is less frilly with a broader leaf; both have dark green outer leaves and creamy blanched hearts.

In seed catalogs, they are usually listed under "endive," and you have to sort out which is which by the descriptions. On the other hand, what we commonly call "endive" or "Belgian endive" is really chicory and is listed that way in catalogs. In the market, "endive" is only "Belgian endive"; chicory and escarole are carefully labeled that way as separate greens. All I can say is thank heaven they put pictures in seed catalogs.

History

It is hard to be absolutely sure the ancient Greeks and Egyptians meant the same thing we do by chicory and escarole, but if they did, these greens were eaten during their time. By the thirteenth century, we know of two kinds grown in Northern Europe, and by the sixteenth century their use had spread throughout the Continent to England. They came to America during the nineteenth century in the familiar forms we know today.

Uses

Although most chicory and escarole goes into the salad bowl, they make excellent cooked vegetables. Italians use them commonly as cooked greens, briefly boiled, and tossed with a little olive oil and garlic.

When to Plant

Since chicory and escarole are exceptionally hardy, it's possible to plant them as soon as the ground can be worked. In practice, however, you would be better advised to grow lettuce in the spring and follow with chicory and escarole for fall harvest. Sow seed about the first of July for best quality and longest-lasting crop.

How to Plant

Seed should be thinly sown ½ inch deep in rows 12″–24″ apart. Barely cover with fine soil firmed so that seeds will not float to the top when watered.

Thinning

Since they grow quite wide, thin plants to 12 inches apart. The thinnings can be eaten or, even better, transplanted. Pick a cloudy or drizzly day, if possible, and water frequently until they have adjusted to their new spot. Even mature plants may wilt slightly on a very hot, sunny day, but water and the cool of evening will revive them completely.

Culture

Fertilize during the growing season and take care to continue to provide ample water. To blanch, tie plant loosely with a soft string when it has reached two-thirds of its maturity. The larger, outer leaves will effectively shade the heart. Pick a spell of dry, sunny days; too much humidity or raindrops trapped inside may rot the heart.

Even if you believe in the greater value of unblanched leaves, don't deprive yourself of the delicious blanched heart; it makes a nice contrast in the salad bowl and there are plenty of dark green leaves for health's sake.

Harvest

Harvest whenever you like. If you leave the plants to maturity, they will provide fresh salad greens late in the fall. They are so hardy that some gardeners have been known to brush the snow aside and pick a head for dinner. Thompson & Morgan says they will stand temperatures as low as 20°F.

Varieties

Chicory seems to arouse a good deal of enthusiasm among seedsmen, if one can judge by the way they describe it in their catalogs. However, it is difficult to distinguish one variety from the other unless you read carefully—"finely cut" generally refers to chicory; "broad-leaved" to escarole.

Thompson & Morgan describes its Sugar Loaf better than I

can: "For most people who get addicted to its delicious fresh flavor, it is without comparison in the winter vegetable kingdom." They and Nichols also have a red-leaved variety; Harris, Nichols, and Stokes offer an "asparagus type" (RADICHETTA) for spring planting and go so far as to say, "Some prefer it to regular asparagus." I've never tried it but it sounds intriguing. Stokes, as usual, has the largest selection; Burpee, "the first seed company in the United States to offer this delicious, different salad crop," limits itself to one variety, SUGARHAT.

Most catalogs no longer list the old standbys, SALAD KING and BROADLEAF BATAVIAN; they are good and reliable if you come upon them.

CHINESE CABBAGE
Brassica pekinensis

Chinese cabbage is not truly a cabbage, although it is a member of the *Brassica* family. It is more closely related to Chinese mustard and, in fact, BOK CHOY, a Chinese mustard commonly found in our produce departments, is often called Chinese cabbage. Since they are both delicious in salads and stir-fry cookery, the confusion in nomenclature is not serious.

If you come upon a vegetable with the lovely name "pe-tsai," that is Chinese cabbage; it is also sometimes called celery cabbage.

History

For once, the name has something to do with the country of origin; Chinese cabbage actually is native to Asia and Japan. It is described in Chinese literature of the fifth century. In the eighteenth century, missionaries returning to Europe brought seeds with them, but it took several introductions over the years before it finally caught on.

Uses

If you are at all into Chinese cooking, you already know how delicious Chinese cabbage is in soups and in wok cookery. It is equally good raw in salads—with radishes and scallions, for instance.

When to Plant

Since Chinese cabbage almost always bolts or goes to seed when planted in the spring, save your energy and wait until July 15th to sow. The garden space can be used in the meantime for radishes, lettuce, beets, carrots, peas, and all the many other vegetables that mature early.

How to Plant

Scatter the seeds thinly as best you can. Cover with 1/2 inch of fine soil. Rows should be 24"–30" apart, depending on the variety. Tall, slender varieties will require less room than short, chunky ones.

Thinning

When 3"–4" high, thin to stand 10 inches apart for tall varieties, 18 inches for short ones. Be sure to use the thinnings in salads for a special treat, or transplant them for a larger crop.

Culture

Happily, this is one plant that is not fussy about soil. Fertilize it, give it plenty of water, and it will thrive. It seems less attractive to pests than true cabbage, although sometimes aphids are a problem. To deter aphids and other pests, grow garlic and shallots in rows between plants.

Harvest

The neat rows of well-shaped Chinese-cabbage heads are a decorative addition to any garden, and when they are mature, you will be reluctant to disturb the symmetry by picking them. If you have planted them in a flower bed, pick every other one for as long as possible.

They may be harvested at all stages of growth but are mature when the heads are firm and no longer increasing in size. Outside leaves should be reserved for soups; the rest can be finely shredded and eaten in many ways.

Chinese cabbage is self-blanching; only the outer leaves will be dark green, and a little coarse for eating raw.

Varieties

Most catalogs offer MICHIHLI, which grows 18 inches tall, 3″– 4″ thick. If you have already tried this and would like to go on to other varieties, Nichols and Thompson & Morgan have some interesting varieties; Burpee has its own hybrids.

WONG BOK is the type most frequently sold in supermarkets: 10 inches tall, 6 inches wide. It keeps better in storage than other varieties.

Don't grow CHIHI; the MICHIHLI is an improved version of it, and there is no reason to go back to the old type.

LETTUCE
Lactuca sativa

More lettuce is consumed than any other single salad ingredient. It is easy to grow and so decorative that once you have grown it in your flower garden, you will never want to be without it. Lettuce makes a beautiful bedding plant, offers a wide range of shades as well as leaf shapes—from the dark green, compact OAK LEAF to the vivid, light green, frilly heads of SALAD BOWL. And there are the beautiful RUBY lettuces to set off light green flower foliage. Add the plus that all this beauty is edible all summer long and you will find lettuce among your flowers irresistible.

History

It is thought by some scholars that all the many forms of lettuce we now grow derived originally from a wild prickly Asian lettuce; however, other forms have been found wild in Asia Minor, Italy, and China. In any case, it is now cultivated in gardens throughout the world and is practically never exported, because each country can grow enough to satisfy its own needs.

Uses

I can't believe that I need to tell anyone how to use lettuce. However, what may be new to you are all the different kinds. Most of the lettuce you see is the type we commonly call "iceberg," and this is looked down upon by gourmets, who prefer the "Boston" type, like BUTTERCRUNCH, or leaf lettuces, like SALAD BOWL. Since they are rarely available in the market, the only way to enjoy these delicious lettuces is to grow them yourself. This can be done in a flowerpot or window box, as well as in the open garden, so you have no excuse for not trying a crop. Lettuce is an easy plant to grow and quick to mature to the eating point.

When to Plant

Since lettuce seed germinates best in a cool temperature, it is easiest to plant in the spring. Get a head start by seeding flats indoors in a cool room; set the seedlings out as soon as possible after the last frost date. Light frosts won't bother them a bit, even though they look so fragile.

If your original planting is large enough, you may need to do only one subsequent planting of leaf lettuce to have enough for the whole season. To do so, don't pick the whole plant; take only the outside leaves. The heart will continue growing and forming more outside leaves, thus providing you with a continuous crop. This won't work, of course, with the heading varieties, since you have to pick the whole head to eat it.

To germinate seed in midsummer, do your best to fool it into thinking it is spring. Pick a cool spell, if possible, to start with; water with very cold water and keep flats out of the sun during the hottest part of the day. I find that lettuces don't need eight hours of sun, so I move the flats into a cool, shady spot fairly early in the day.

How to Plant

Slightly basic, or alkaline (around 6.0) soil is best; otherwise any good garden soil will do. It should be well drained, because lettuce requires more water than most vegetables but doesn't like wet feet. Surprisingly enough, it likes frequent light fertilizing. A mulch of wood ashes covered with sand will give you especially good results; the wood ashes will furnish the extra potash lettuce needs and the sand will keep the bottom leaves from rotting.

If you don't want to bother with transplanting—and most of the time it's not worth the extra work with such a fast-maturing crop—sow seeds 1/4"–1/2" deep, about 18 inches between rows. Head lettuce and romaine require slightly less room; about 12 inches should do it.

Since lettuce has a tendency to bolt in really hot weather, you may need to sow a second crop in midsummer. The best way to do this is to keep the seedbed watered with the coldest water you have; ice water is good. Mist three times a day to keep the soil cool. As I mentioned earlier, lettuce is supposed to do best in full sun, but I find summer lettuce grows better in the shade of a taller plant; WITLOOF CHICORY makes a fine small hedge to grow lettuce behind.

Once the seeds have germinated and formed true leaves, discontinue the very cold water. But it is always good practice to water lettuce last when the coldest water has had a chance to come through the pipes; other plants don't like the shock of cold water on a hot summer day, so save it for lettuce, which does.

Culture

If you water frequently—and you can't depend on normal rainfall with lettuce—and fertilize lightly with a 5–10–10 fertilizer, you will find lettuce less trouble to grow than any crop except radishes.

Harvest

Leaf lettuce can be harvested all season long by picking the outside leaves. Some gardeners say this is not good practice, but I don't know why; it works for me. Head lettuce should be harvested anytime after the head has formed and is firm; this applies to Bibb as well as to the crisp iceberg types. In practice, I tend to let them get too mature, because they look so pretty I hate to pick them; to enjoy them at their peak, don't wait that long.

Varieties

Before we can discuss specific varieties, we need to know the various types of lettuces. I think it's clearest if we divide lettuce into four types:

1. *Crisphead.* The "iceberg" type most commonly found in the market.
2. *Butterhead.* A familiar example is the kind sold as "Boston."
3. *Romaine.* Sold as romaine.
4. *Leaf Lettuce.* If you're lucky enough to find it in the market at all, it will usually be SALAD BOWL.

There are so many varieties of these different types that you could get hooked on just growing a special lettuce garden to try them all out—a different group each summer. Stokes lists twenty-four varieties; Burpee eighteen. Some of the catalogs with fewer listings offer unusual varieties not found in the other catalogs.

In addition to the four types listed, you should know of two special types of lettuce. The midget lettuces, excellent for small gardens and containers, are often found in catalogs on a special page of midget vegetables, instead of listed with other lettuces. If you are interested in this kind, be sure to hunt for it. The other type is a red or bronze leaf lettuce. This is a beautiful lettuce, but it can be disappointing if you have your heart set on RUBY, the best and reddest variety. Of the several times I've ordered it, only once did I actually get it; all the other times the crop either failed or the seeds were all gone. If you want it, order early; if you don't get RUBY, the seedsman will probably send you the closest thing he has to it.

Now to specific varieties—these are only a few suggestions. There are many, many more good ones.

SOME SUGGESTED VARIETIES

Crisphead
GREAT LAKES.
IMPERIAL.
PENNLAKE.

Butterhead

BUTTERCRUNCH. Rated in the Thompson & Morgan *Eating Guide* as "Supreme," a rating they seldom give. Do try this one.

TOM THUMB. A midget—about the only one offered.

BUTTER KING.

Leaf

BLACK SEEDED SIMPSON.

SALAD BOWL.

OAKLEAF.

GRAND RAPIDS.

Red Leaf

RUBY.

PRIZEHEAD.

Cos or Romaine

PARIS WHITE. Most commonly offered.

DARK GREEN COS.

PARRIS ISLAND.

TRIANON.

SPINACH
Spinacia oleracea

In the old days, spinach was often urged on children (who disliked it intensely) because it was thought to be so good for them. Now some authorities actually warn us off spinach because of its high oxalic-acid content. Naturally, once we are not urged to eat it, we have suddenly discovered it is delicious, especially eaten raw in salads, and almost everyone, including children, likes it that way. On balance, I think the good in spinach far outweighs the bad, and as an ingredient in spinach pie or tossed salads, it certainly can't be beat.

If the oxalic-acid content worries you, Thompson & Morgan offers a new spinach with a low oxalic-acid content.

History

Spinach was apparently unknown except in a few Mediterranean countries until comparatively recent times. However, the Moors finally introduced it to Spain and it reached China by way of Nepal, so that by the eighteenth century it was even growing in our own Colonial gardens; now it is widely cultivated throughout the world.

When to Plant

Spinach is finicky about temperatures. If you have a normal spring with cold weather gradually turning into warm, spinach will go to seed as soon as the warm days lengthen. Fortunately, we almost never have a normal spring, and it is usually possible to raise a fairly good crop before the really hot weather is upon us. In the summer, you can switch over to the so-called "summer spinach"—not true spinach but acceptable substitutes. If you wish to grow these, look for directions for NEW ZEALAND SPINACH, MALABAR, and TAMPALA.

Spinach should be planted as soon as the ground can be worked, or in late summer for a late-fall crop.

How to Plant

Seed should be sown about ½ inch deep in rows 12″–18″ apart. Plants should stand 4″–6″ apart. Let the seedlings grow until you are sure which ones are sturdy; then thin if necessary, and eat the thinnings.

Culture

Spinach likes a lot of water and is one of the few vegetables, I feel, that benefit from overhead watering. If you use a commercial 5–10–10 fertilizer, add extra nitrogen, or use 10–10–10 to begin with.

Harvest

Pick spinach anytime you need it. I eat it mostly raw, so I usually go out and pick whatever I need a few hours before a meal. This gives me time to wash it thoroughly and put it aside in the refrigerator. I prefer immature leaves, so my spinach never bolts; it just doesn't get a chance.

If you think your spinach is almost mature and if it looks as though a really hot spell is coming, pick it all. Once it bolts, it's not worth eating. With fall spinach, watch out for early frost.

VARIETIES

Spring/Fall
BLOOMSDALE LONG STANDING.
WINTER BLOOMSDALE.
VIKING.
AMERICA.
NOBEL or GIANT THICK-LEAVED.

Fall Only
VIRGINIA SAVOY.
HYBRID NO. 7.
DIXIE MARKET.

Low Oxalic Acid
MANNOPE. This is new, and Thompson & Morgan is the only catalog I know of that offers it.

SUMMER SPINACH

Once you have tasted the delights of raw spinach, you will want to have it in your garden all season. Since this is not practical with true spinach, spinach lovers can grow acceptable substitutes: NEW ZEALAND SPINACH; MALABAR SPINACH; TAMPALA. These all taste something like spinach and will withstand summer heat.

When to Plant

These are warm-weather vegetables and should not be planted until all danger of frost is past.

How to Plant

Seeds are slow to germinate; soak them twenty-four hours in warm water and plant immediately.

NEW ZEALAND SPINACH grows as a vine. Seeds should be planted 1½ inches deep, 18 inches apart, in rows 24 inches apart.

MALABAR is also a vine. Sow seeds ½ inch deep, 12 inches apart, in rows 12 inches apart.

TAMPALA should be sown ¼"–½" deep, 4"–6" apart, in rows 24"–30" apart.

All vines can be trained up a fence to save garden space.

Culture

Summer spinach is easy to grow, similar in culture to true spinach. Water generously and provide extra nitrogen.

Harvest

Summer spinach can be cropped all summer. If you do not take too much from any one plant and give it time to recover and send out new tips after cropping, you will have a steady supply the whole season. The young leaves are the only good part, so constant cropping works best.

Varieties

There is no choice, just one listing for each, and not all catalogs list TAMPALA. Nichols lists one other, HOJO SPINACH, "widely grown in the Northern provinces of Japan where it is highly prized . . ." I have never tried it, but you might like to.

WATERCRESS
Nasturtium officinale

Since I like to eat large quantities of watercress in salads and sandwiches, I have always been frustrated by the price of the small, damp bunches available in the marketplace. However, there is no running brook on our small acreage, so I thought I couldn't grow my own. Happily, running water is not absolutely essential; watercress is grown commercially in greenhouses, and you can easily grow it in your garden or house if you meet its fairly simple requirements.

History

For over two thousand years, man has used watercress both for food and as medicine; it is equally valued for both purposes even at the present time.

Although not native to America, it was introduced to this

continent by the early explorers and soon adapted itself to wooded brooks and streams. Unfortunately, it often grows together with fool's cress, or marshwort, which is poisonous, so it should not be gathered in the wild unless you are sure you know the difference.

Watercress is as good for you as it is delicious; it is rich in iodine and very high in vitamin C. In addition, it is supposed to be effective when applied to certain types of acne and has been used, on occasion, as a specific for tuberculosis (although I wouldn't recommend it). It is also supposed to improve the appetite, but in spite of this, it is a favorite of dieters because it contains no calories. In a salt-free diet, its peppery, spicy taste adds interest to salads and sandwiches.

When to Plant

Watercress can be planted in the house whenever you please, or outdoors during April and May. It is a perennial, so once you have a good stand of it, it will grow nicely without any special care and will spread into whatever space suits it.

How to Plant

You can buy a bunch in the market (be sure it is fresh and dark green, without yellowed or withered leaves) and cut it into pieces; it will root at every joint. The cuttings should be put into pots of Cornell Mix with a teaspoonful of limestone mixed in thoroughly. Keep in a shady spot and keep moist; it roots easily.

To grow from seed—and almost every seed catalog offers watercress—spread thinly $1/4$ inch deep, 1 inch apart in pots of the same mixture as for cuttings. If your house is dry, cover the pots lightly with plastic so the top soil does not dry out between waterings.

With either method, you will have greater success if you set your pots in water.

Culture

When your watercress cuttings have taken root, or your seedlings are 2″–3″ tall, set them out 1 inch apart in a damp, shady place in the garden (a little sun is tolerated, but it should be filtered through leaves), or on the side of a stream where the soil is always damp. If they are planted in the garden, the soil should be generously incorporated with peat moss, but well limed, since watercress does best in a soil rich in calcium.

Because it grows naturally in a running stream, watercress likes cool, or even cold, water. If you are going to be away and plan to wick-water your plants, use ice cubes instead of water; as they melt, the wick will pick up the cold water and your watercress will thrive. (Of course, if you're going to be away very long, this won't work, but in that case, you will probably turn the heat down anyway.) A saucer filled with crushed ice will also serve for a time.

Bottom-watering will eventually result in a slightly foamy top to the water in the pot. I have never heard that this is harmful but I can't think it is particularly good for the plant, so every so often I top-water it and run off the foam. It's not much trouble and I have had such good success with my watercress that I think it is worth it; the closer you imitate a running brook the better.

Harvest

Cut your watercress whenever you want so long as you leave the plants enough to grow on. However, if you want to take cuttings for propagation, spring and fall are the best times.

Varieties

I have never seen any special varieties of watercress offered; it is not identified in any particular way but is usually described as "improved."

I often just pick up a bunch at the market, rather than waiting for the seeds to get to cutting size. Actually there is no reason why you should ever have to plant watercress from commercial sources more than once, but if you are like me, you are bound to let the plants dry out sometime and find it necessary to start over again. It's so easy it really doesn't matter if that happens.

Cautionary Note

Unfortunately, in these polluted times, a sparkling brook running through your property may not be as clean as it looks. If you are planning to plant your watercress there, have the water tested.

CHAPTER FIVE

How to Grow
Cucumbers and Other
Crunchy Things

WHILE GREENS ARE the foundation of most salads, the difference in texture provided by crunchy ingredients is a welcome change of pace. Recent studies (the subjects chosen for studies are endlessly amazing to me) have shown that the "crunch" itself is an important ingredient in the enjoyment of crisp vegetables—so much for the years recently devoted to the development of a "crunchless" cucumber. Thank goodness they never succeeded in this endeavor, and today the only crunchless cucumber is an overcooked one.

CARROTS
Daucus carota

If you have never eaten carrots right out of the garden, you don't really know what a carrot tastes like. Your first experience of a fresh-picked baby carrot washed in cold well water and eaten out of hand is as wonderful as your first taste of lobster (always assuming you liked the lobster). The tired, topless grocery carrot, the rigid orange stumps in the store freezer—even the pseudo-gastronomic delights of the canned Belgian baby carrots —are different, vastly inferior vegetables. Eating raw carrots, you will understand why Indian children had to be restrained from slipping into the garden to steal the young carrots.

History

The carrot was well known to the ancient Greeks and Romans and its culture gradually spread throughout the civilized world. It had both culinary and medicinal uses, and was thought to be good for stomach disorders, as well as for the kidneys and the intestines; today it is considered useful in the treatment of night blindness and other eye ailments. Carrots were grown in the gardens of the Jamestown, Virginia, and Massachusetts Bay colonies, and were adopted by the Indians, who esteemed them highly.

The first cultivated carrots were purple, occasionally white, and can be seen, faithfully delineated in those colors, in eighteenth-century Dutch paintings. Early in that century, the Dutch developed the orange carrot we know today, adding immeasurably to our nutrition; the orange carrot is an excellent source of vitamin A (one of the few sources that are not loaded with saturated fats), as well as B_1, C, and calcium.

Uses

Carrots are good grated or sliced in a tossed salad, served as *crudités* in the form of carrot sticks, and excellent marinated or pickled for the hors-d'oeuvre tray. Because of their sweetness, they have great appeal for children and can easily be used to replace less wholesome snacks. They are an essential ingredient in most stews and lend themselves to a tremendous variety of dishes, including cake.

In the time of James I of England, carrot foliage was used in corsages and flower arrangements much as baby's-breath was twenty years ago. The feathery light green foliage is very decorative in container gardening and indoor herb gardens, even if the container does not have sufficient depth to grow it to maturity.

When to Plant

Carrots are hardy and can be planted as early as the ground can be worked.

How to Plant

The seeds are tiny and very slow—two to three weeks—to germinate. Mix them with sand and dribble along the row, then cover with ¼ inch of fine, firmed soil. A common practice is to intersow with radish seeds. The radishes germinate quickly, help to mark the row, and come to maturity when the carrots are barely showing. Pull the radishes, thus loosening the soil to the advantage of the tender carrot roots, firm the soil gently, and water well. Rows should be about 14 inches apart.

Resow carrots every two to three weeks for a steady supply.

Thinning

Carrot seeds are too small to plant one at a time, so you will have to thin the seedlings. They should stand about 1½ inches apart in rows 12″–14″ apart, but can be closer if you plan to pull every other one as a baby carrot. This is a very satisfactory way of thinning, because you make maximum use of your space—and at the same time give yourself a rare treat.

Culture

Outside of mulching, which is a good idea for any vegetable, carrots require very little care. Mulching is necessary because carrots are particularly unaggressive plants and cannot compete with weeds. It also prevents the soil from crusting while waiting for the seeds to germinate. Water normally and you will probably have no problems.

Harvest

When you use carrots is a matter of taste. They can be harvested from the time they are an inch long until they reach their full growth. In general, there is no reason for the home gardener to wait until they reach maturity unless he wants to store them for winter use. Otherwise the young carrots are even more delicious than the mature ones and should be enjoyed as a treat money can't buy.

Varieties

Carrots come in all sizes and shapes. The Burpee catalog has a very helpful line drawing of the shapes of varieties, so that you can see what you are ordering. Home gardeners are better off with the short-rooted varieties, which do not require that the soil be deeply prepared.

In general, I avoid any variety developed for comercial use. If, for instance, a carrot is described as "for market, home garden, and shipping," I pass it by. On the other hand, if it says, "too tender to be a good shipper," I make a note of it. Basically you will do well with any carrot with "Nantes" in its name, whereas you may want to avoid the IMPERATORS and CHANTENAY ROYALS, varieties often found at the supermarket. However, read your description carefully; the seedsman may have developed a good commercial strain of Nantes, and you might want to *avoid* that particular carrot.

Thompson & Morgan lists carrots that have been developed in England. FRUBAND is a good one. Burrell lists NANTES IMPROVED CORELESS, as do several other catalogs. Burpee has GOLDINHART and LITTLE FINGER, which are exceptional.

An interesting carrot to grow is the round, beet-shaped orange carrot. Thompson & Morgan's KONFRIX is a good one. However, this year they ran out of seed; order early if you want to be sure of getting what you specify—and even then you may not if the crop has failed.

Since carrots are sowed several times during the season, take a chance on the Nichols BELGIUM WHITE CARROT. A dish of white and orange carrot sticks would look great on a summer buffet. You might also want to try a carrot from France, PRIME-NANTES.

CELERY
Apium graveolens

Celery has come a long way from the wild plant the Romans harvested in swampy areas. Its originally strong, bitter flavor has been tamed, and it has adapted to drier growing conditions. Since any respectable salad maker will sooner or later need celery, you may want to try your hand at growing it.

History

The wild celery plant was the only kind known to early civilizations. Since it grew freely and was easy to harvest, it was used

—though primarily for medicinal purposes—from early times. It probably originated around the Mediterranean, but has been found in its wild state from southern Asia to most parts of Europe. Some early writings on the subject say "celery" when they really mean "rock celery"—our parsley.

Uses

There is no need to tell anyone the many ways to use raw celery, although stuffed celery stalks have, to a large extent, become the standard fare at parties. Braised celery is a delicious dish that you should try if you haven't already; cream of celery soup should be a house specialty.

When to Plant

Celery has a reputation for being difficult. Many garden books will state flatly that it is too hard for the home gardener. This sort of remark brings out my sporting blood, and I promptly include the vegetable in next year's garden plan. Actually, part of the problem with celery is that it has a long growing season, yet is fussy about temperatures. With our changeable New England weather, anything fussy has hard going. I have had very good luck with celery, so try it and see how you make out.

Plant it indoors in February or March to get an early-spring start, or buy plants from your local nursery; otherwise, hot weather will cause it to bolt. Plants, whether home-grown or bought, should not be set out in the open garden until all danger of frost is past. If it is an exceptionally cool, wet spring, delay setting out. If this is impractical, plant in July for a fall crop.

How to Plant

Celery seed is almost as slow-germinating as parsley. Soak the seed in warm water overnight and plant immediately next morning. The seed is very fine, so drain it through a sieve. (Don't use cheesecloth, or you will spend the whole morning trying to pick out the seeds.)

Sow seeds $\frac{1}{8}$ inch deep in flats of Cornell Mix 1 inch apart in rows 2 inches apart. Just sprinkle with enough mix to cover; water from the bottom until the surface is thoroughly damp. Do not let the soil float or the seeds may float to the top and dry out instead of germinating. *If you wet the mix thoroughly before filling your flat, it works even better.* Then sprinkle with dry mix to cover the seeds and press gently with a board until the dry mix has absorbed all the moisture it can.

Seedlings should appear in two to three weeks, during which time never allow the soil to dry out.

Transplant about four weeks later; to transplant, seedlings should be sturdy enough to stand 2 inches apart. Four more weeks and you can set them in the garden 8 inches apart in rows at least 24 inches apart. Set them the same depth they were growing in the flat.

Tip

One way to keep the soil moist is to cover it with moist burlap until the tiny green leaves appear. Keep the burlap well misted and you will seldom, if ever, have to water the soil. Don't get absent-minded about it, however; the burlap must be removed as soon as any growth appears. Check the soil occasionally in case it needs a booster watering.

Thinning

With all the transplanting celery requires, you never have to thin. And, of course, if you buy plants, set them out the proper distance first time around.

Culture

Celery is a heavy feeder and a heavy drinker. Regular and frequent (but always light) applications of 5–10–10 are necessary, as well as regular watering. However, do not allow the soil to become soggy, or the plants will rot or be more subject to disease. Celery likes plenty of manure and compost or other humus in its soil, so be sure your soil is properly prepared before you set out the plants.

Blanching

As life becomes more complicated and busier, some of the "refinements" of living fall by the wayside. Blanching celery is one of these. Nutritionists tell us green celery is better for us; gardeners find the time taken to blanch celery is better spent putting in another row of beets; gourmets find the taste of unblanched celery is really excellent.

All in all, why bother blanching? But if you feel you must, celery can be blanched between two boards, or the stalks can be individually foil-wrapped; anything that shades the stalks from the sun will blanch them. This should be done when the plant is about two-thirds toward maturity.

There is a variety of celery that is supposed to be self-blanching, but I have never grown it.

Harvest

Cut celery as you need it. Pick it all before frost or mulch it heavily with straw and harvest up until December. I like to pick it before it is fully mature; the delicate taste of the heart then extends to the larger stalks and is particularly delicious.

Do, by the way, use the leaves. They are just as good as the stalks.

Varieties

GOLDEN SELF-BLANCHING, UTAH, and GOLDEN PLUME are all considered good and are found in the greatest number of catalogs. The PASCALS are reliable old favorites. Stokes has the largest selection—nine varieties. Thompson & Morgan, as always, has some unusual varieties; Gurney has a red celery that I don't know anything about, but it might be fun to try.

CUCUMBER
Cucumis sativus

It wouldn't be a respectable relish tray without cucumbers, and their popularity with home gardeners is evident when you look at the seed offerings; almost every catalog lists at least ten to twelve varieties. Gurney provides color photographs of nineteen varieties, along with further listings; Stokes offers over thirty different varieties. Since you can grow cucumbers easily in containers, as well as in the open garden, there is always room for them. Have fun!

History

Long before horticultural records existed, the cucumber was grown in India and the East Indies. We do not know exactly how it originated, since it has never been found growing wild; the so-called "wild cucumber," though edible, is not related.

The Romans were so fond of cucumbers that they developed a highly sophisticated method for growing them out of season, and the Emperor Tiberius took advantage of this feat to eat them every single day throughout the year.

Charlemagne included them in his imperial vegetable garden, and Columbus considered them worthy of bringing to the West

Indies. Early colonists in Virginia and Massachusetts grew them, and introduced them to the Indians, who spread them even farther afield.

Most of the varieties we grow today are identical with those grown in ancient times—with the exceptions of hybrids, which are mainly improvements on old varieties.

Uses

The crisp goodness of cucumbers in salads is one of the mainstays of every hostess, and their relatively low cost makes them available to all. A few vines will supply a large family; they are very prolific. It is unfortunate that market cucumbers are so heavily waxed as to be downright unappetizing; if you grow your own, you won't have this problem.

Nothing is more delicious raw than a home-grown cucumber. Slice into one in your kitchen and its fragrance will fill the house.

Cucumbers are grown in gardens everywhere, from China to Europe to the United States, an integral part of every country's cuisine. If the only way you have ever tasted them is raw, try them cooked; they are completely, deliciously different, and much more digestible.

When to Plant

Cucumbers are very sensitive to cold and do best if planted when the ground has completely warmed up, so when to plant depends partly on the kind of spring you have. One year I couldn't plant them until the second week in June; another year I got them in in May.

How to Plant

Prepare the soil with plenty of well-rotted or dried manure, peat moss, and fertilizer. Keep the top 2 inches free of this mixture, but be sure the richer soil extends 12″–18″ beneath the hills.

Hills—or large, shallow, saucerlike depressions in the open garden—should contain five or six seeds. Plant them about 2 inches apart in a circle and cover with 1 inch of fine, firmed soil. The hills should stand about 4′–6′ apart.

Or plant in containers. A box or basket of lemon cucumbers on the patio is beautifully decorative and delightfully useful.

Thinning

When you are sure how many good healthy plants you have, thin down to the best two or three to a hill.

Culture

Cucumbers aren't difficult to grow so long as you give them plenty of water. The best way is to water them thoroughly, then mulch with hay or straw. Do not let the mulch actually touch the main stems but get as close as you can. From then on, water right through the mulch.

If space is limited, or even if it is not, grow cucumbers up a fence, or on chicken wire stapled to two stakes between the hills; the fruit will grow beautifully straight and be much less subject to disease. It will also be easier to find and pick.

When the first flowers appear, fertilize again and every three or four weeks thereafter.

Some gardeners do a second planting for an all-season crop; I always find my original planting produces madly until killed by frost.

Many gardeners are disappointed when the first flowers don't seem to produce any fruit. That happens because the first flowers are male, and it isn't until female flowers appear that cucumbers start to form. Once they do start, they grow overnight.

When the main vine stem gets as long as the top of your fence, or the area you have allotted to it, pinch off the tip. The vine will stop growing in length and put its energy into growing laterals, which will produce heavy yields. The laterals can be trained on the fence just like the main stem.

If you are very impatient and want to get the earliest possible fruit, grow the all-female-flowered, or gynoecious, varieties. I don't think they produce any more fruit in the long run, but since the very first flowers can set fruit, you may have cucumbers before anyone else in your area. These cukes have much fewer and finer seeds than male-female flowering plants; they are, therefore, "burpless," and can be tolerated by people who get uncomfortable feelings after eating regular ones.

Tip

Although cucumbers grow so fast you will have trouble keeping up with them, you must do so. Once a vine has developed a fully ripe cucumber (it will turn yellow rather than dark green), it will consider that its work is done and will stop bearing; you might as well pull up the vine if that happens and use the space for something else. So be sure to keep picking, even if your refrigerator is bursting with cucumbers. (The yellow color as an indication of overripeness does not, of course, apply to the lemon cucumber.)

Varieties

As I indicated in the opening paragraph, there are enough cucumber varieties to make you dizzy. The gynoecious ones include: PIONEER, SHAMROCK, VICTORY, SWEET SLICE, and GEMINI.

For container gardenings, try PATIO PIK, which grows 7-inch cucumbers on dwarf vines that spread only 18″–24″ and can be trellised or grown up a chicken-wire circle from a basket container. Or TINY DILL CUKE, which has 2-inch finger-length fruit.

If you want gherkins to pickle, don't settle for immature regular cucumbers; grow the real thing—the WEST INDIES GHERKIN, which is prickly and the only true gherkin. It makes great pickles but is not especially good raw.

For novelty and a new taste and look in your salads, LEMON CUCUMBER, which is actually the size, shape, and color of a large lemon, is great fun. It's sweet and very pretty on the vine as well as on the table.

For those lucky enough to have a greenhouse, there is a whole special world of greenhouse cucumbers, which can't be grown out of doors. They are long, narrow, and seedless and are identified as greenhouse or "European" cucumbers; the English are very fond of them. In addition, there are the long, slim "China" cucumbers, which can be sliced and eaten out of hand without ever peeling.

I've been putting off telling you about the regular varieties because there is such a long list: GEMINI HYBRID, POINSETT, BURPEE HYBRID, ASHLEY, MARKETMORE, MARKETER HYBRID, TRIUMPH, and, as if your cup weren't already running over, a white variety called WHITE WONDER. I've chosen these varieties rather arbitrarily, because they can be found in the greatest number of catalogs, but there are many, many more.

PEPPER
Capiscum frutescens

When we say peppers, most of us think of the sweet green bell peppers we use for stuffing and in salads, but there is a whole world of peppers open to the home gardener. You can grow green, red, or yellow peppers, all shapes and sizes, mild as milk or numbingly hot. You can make your own chili powder, fill your freezer with chopped sweet green and red peppers for winter casseroles, dry whole peppers in decorative strings to hang in your kitchen, and have the prettiest patio in the county with pepper plants in containers.

History

Peppers apparently originated in South America, which is why so many peppers are called "chiles" or "chilis." They have been found in Peruvian ruins and in embroidery or drawings on Indian artifacts dating back two thousand years. Man has always had a spicy tooth as well as a sweet one, and even today hot peppers are eaten in enormous quantities by Mexicans, the people of India, and in certain provinces in China; hot peppers are an essential ingredient of curry, chili, and Szechwan dishes.

Columbus, looking for the black pepper of the Far East, found instead the wonderfully hot and spicy peppers of the West Indies, and they were warmly welcomed in Europe. In the seventeenth century, the Portuguese introduced them to India and Asia where they became so widely grown that early botanists thought they had originated there. Paprika, Tabasco, and pimiento are all peppers; black and white pepper is from an entirely different plant.

Uses

Sweet peppers are good both raw and cooked, and freeze well. Hot peppers can be used fresh or dried. There are special peppers, such as the cherry peppers, that are delicious pickled whole.

When to Plant

Since peppers are very, very sensitive to cold, you will either have to start them indoors or buy plants locally. If you wish to grow only the sweet peppers and the frying peppers, plants can usually be found where tomato plants are offered. However, if you wish to grow CAYENNE, SWEET BANANA, HUNGARIAN WAX, or any other out-of-the-ordinary peppers, start them yourself indoors about six to eight weeks before the time the soil in your area will have warmed up. If you put them out sooner, you may, at worst, lose all your plants; at best, they will just sit there and shiver and not do well even when they finally get warm.

How to Plant

Sow seeds indoors in Cornell Mix–type soil and keep well watered. Sow ¼ inch deep, about 2 inches apart for easy transplanting. The seeds will take a couple of weeks to germinate, so don't get impatient.

In six to eight weeks, seedlings will be large enough and sturdy enough to plant outside with proper hardening. Set plants 18″–24″ apart in rows 24″–36″ apart, depending on the variety.

Culture

Mulch well to eliminate weeding, and fertilize when blossoms first appear. Water if rainfall is erratic or slight.

Harvest

Study the directions for the particular variety you are growing. Some peppers can be harvested green when large enough to suit your purpose; some can be allowed to turn from green to red (merely a maturing process), if you happen to prefer that color. There are peppers that are yellow when they are ripe, and all sorts of other variations.

Many peppers should be picked as soon as they are mature, or the plant will think it has finished its job and will stop bearing. Hot peppers for drying must always be allowed to mature fully.

VARIETIES

Bell and Other Sweet Peppers
 CANAPE.
 EARLY BOUNTIFUL.
 CALIFORNIA WONDER.
 SWEET BANANA.
 GOLDEN CALWONDER.

Hot
 LONG RED CAYENNE.
 HUNGARIAN WAX.
 JALAPENO.
 ANAHEIM CHILI.
 RED CHILI.

Frying
 CUBANELLE.

A note about an unusual new sweet pepper that is not bell-shaped: Thompson & Morgan offers SLIM PIM, which I have not yet tried but which looks and sounds very interesting.

RADISH
Raphanus sativus

If radishes were expensive, we would value them as a rare, pungent vegetable. They are beautiful to look at, crisp and delicious to eat, and much more versatile than the few ways we usually serve them.

History

The radish takes its name from the Sanskrit word *"rudhira"* or "blood," a reference to red radishes; in the Far East today white radishes are actually much more common.

It is a very ancient vegetable and, while once thought of as strictly workingman's fare (along with watercress), it has its more aristocratic side also. In France, it merits a separate course, and in China it is one of the few vegetables served raw in salads and used for their intricate vegetable sculptures.

Although radish contains practically no calories, it is high in vitamin C. The ancient Egyptians thought it increased physical strength, so they fed it in great quantities to the builders of the great pyramids. The Greeks fashioned solid-gold radishes as offerings to Apollo, the Sun God, and the Romans probably introduced them to Britain. In any case, they were well enough known there by the seventeenth century for the early-American colonists to include them in their kitchen gardens.

Uses

Commonly served as finger food along with celery and olives, radishes are familiar to almost everyone. It is not generally known, however, that the seeds are also edible, and can be eaten raw, or pickled like capers. For a real change, try cooking sliced, buttered radishes briefly—an excellent way to use those that have got a little past their prime for eating out of hand.

When to Plant

There are two kinds of radishes; spring/summer, and fall/winter. Spring/summer radishes can be sowed as early as the ground can be worked. They don't thrive in really hot weather, but since they mature in two to three weeks, it's worth a try to keep growing them right through the summer. Fall/winter radishes grow more slowly and should be planted from July 15th on, depending on the variety; some varieties mature in 75 days, some take only 50.

How to Plant

Take an extra minute to plant seeds 1½″–2″ apart and save yourself the bother of thinning. The seeds are large and round and easy to handle, so there is no reason to drop them helter-skelter into the drill.

Sow ½ inch deep in rows 6″–12″ apart. Larger radishes need more room; allow up to 12 inches between the really tremendous Oriental kinds.

Culture

Radishes are so easy to grow they are one of the first things in children's gardens. A normally fertile, friable soil, with a little extra phosphate added, will give you a good crop. Fertilize again each time you plant.

Harvest

When the radish is large enough to eat, the shoulder usually shows a little above the ground. If you are still not sure, take some earth away from the stem; if the root looks too small, push back the earth, firm it around the stem, and wait a bit.

Varieties

Radishes come red, white, yellow, black, or violet; in choosing varieties make sure you are ordering the kind you want. Also, as we have mentioned before, there are "regular" radishes and the late-fall/winter varieties, which require different culture and have quite different flavors. No matter what color the radish skin, the flesh is usually white.

VARIETIES

Spring/Summer Red
CHERRY BELLE.
CRIMSON GIANT.
CHAMPION.
FRENCH BREAKFAST.

Spring/Summer White
BURPEE WHITE.
ICICLE.
COMET.

Spring/Summer Yellow
Gurney has one they just describe as "yellow radish"; Thompson & Morgan has one they rave about called YELLOW GOLD.

Fall/Winter Black
ROUND BLACK SPANISH.
LONG BLACK SPANISH.

Fall/Winter White
CHINESE WHITE.
WHITE STRASBURG.
TAKINASHI. Mostly for cooking.
SAKURAJIMA MAMMOTH. Has grown to 100 lbs. in weight in Japan—used for cooking and vegetable sculpture. Only Nichols carries it, so far as I know.

Fall/Winter Red
CHINA ROSE.

Fall/Winter Violet
RADISH DE GOURNAY. From Nichols.

BEAN SPROUTS

I like to nibble on a bowl of bean or seed sprouts just as I like to munch carrot sticks. They're better for you than popcorn or potato chips and can be just as addictive.

If you grow your own, so that they are always fresh and crisp, you'll find dozens of ways to use them. Mung beans are the traditional beans to use and the easiest to sprout, but some of the others may be even more to your taste.

Uses

Bean sprouts are a surprisingly versatile vegetable. In Chinese cuisine, they are used both raw in salads and hot in soups and stir-fry cookery. They are excellent for egg-roll filling (though not used alone) . In cooking with them, the secret is merely to heat them through so that they do not lose their crispness.

When to Plant

Since bean sprouts are grown indoors and can be ready to eat in two to five days, start them a few days before you want to use them. They are best when fresh, so keep a crop coming rather than storing a supply in your refrigerator for any length of time.

How to Plant

Actually, you don't "plant" them, since no soil is involved. You can grow them in commercial containers called "bean sprouters"; they take up comparatively little room and are attractive on counter or windowsill. Wide-mouthed Mason jars are popular and inexpensive sprouters; just follow the same directions whatever container you use.

To Sprout

All you need is moisture—no soil, no fertilizer.

Soak beans in warm water overnight. Then put several layers of damp paper toweling on the bottom of the jar and lay the drained beans on it. Cover the top of the jar with two layers of damp cheesecloth secured with a rubber band. It is important for air to circulate freely within the growing area.

Keep the seeds *moist but not wet.* If they dry out, they will wither; if they are too wet, they will rot. Rinse with fresh water and drain twice a day, replacing toweling.

Culture

The seeds will take care of themselves if conditions are right. Seeds sprouted in a light but not sunny window will be greener than those sprouted on the kitchen counter or in the dark. Naturally, green ones have more nutrients (but less vitamin C) ; however, you may prefer the taste of the white sprouts. Both are so rich in nutrients that it is more important to grow the kind you like—and will therefore eat more of—than to stoically grow the kind that are better for you but that you won't enjoy.

Varieties

Only the Burpee catalog bothers to list a specific variety; they offer a mung bean, BERKEN. Nichols gives no specific varieties but lists mung beans, alfalfa, red clover, peppergrass, black radish, and lentils.

Thompson & Morgan has the most intriguing selections: SPICY FENUGREEKS, NATURAL TRITICALE, and a mixture they call SALAD SPROUTS, plus mung beans. The catalog illustrates every one in full color, which is very helpful.

Since bean sprouts vary considerably in flavor, don't give

them up because you don't like the first variety you grow; especially don't start with soybean sprouts—they are the least popular, although some people doggedly stick with them because they are the cheapest. Mung beans are usually the most expensive but they have the finest flavor, and I'd rather eat a smaller quantity and enjoy my meal. Anyhow, food is supposed to do you more good if you enjoy it.

Caution

Do not eat potato sprouts; they are poisonous. And do not use seeds ordered for planting; they may be treated with fungicide.

CHAPTER SIX

A Few Herbs for the Salad Bowl

THERE ARE MANY marvelous herbs, and almost all of them are good in salads. Although this chapter includes only anise, dill, fennel, and parsley, you will find many more in the recipe section.

If you want to explore the possibilities of herbs you are not familiar with, don't hesitate to experiment. Take a little of the herb, mince and blend with butter, then spread on an unsalted cracker or a bit of white bread; you will know at once whether you want to try it in your salads.

Although most herbs are easy to grow, each has its own special requirements, which must be heeded. Some are annuals, some are perennials (though not all perennials do well the second year) ; many are not winter hardy and must be brought indoors for the winter. All herbs can be grown indoors or in containers.

ANISE
Pimpinella anisum

Anise is sometimes called "aniseed" and "sweet cumin," but it should not be confused with true cumin (*Cuminum cyminum*), which, although also a member of the carrot family, is a completely different plant. Star anise, often called for in Chinese cookery, is also a different plant.

Anise is a pretty plant, with bright green feathery foliage and attractive white flowers. If you want to put it in the flower border, put it in back of ageratum, dwarf marigolds, and other low-growing annuals, as it grows 18"–24" high. It is an annual and will have to be started from seed each spring. It is particularly successful with flowers like petunias and zinnias, which also thrive under fairly dry conditions.

History

Anise originated in the lands around the Mediterranean and is now widely grown throughout the world. Its culinary and medicinal use goes back at least as far as ancient Egypt where it was an ingredient in embalming fluid as well as a kitchen herb.

The ancient Greeks and Romans cultivated it both for its delicious flavor and as a medicine. They ate it in the form of Mustace, a spice cake that was served at the end of a feast to ward off indigestion and to renew the appetite. By the Middle Ages, it was known in Central Europe and Charlemagne was very fond of it.

Today it is widely grown for export throughout the Temperate Zone, including such countries as Turkey, Mexico, Spain, India, and Italy, and parts of South America. Still used medicinally, it is found in paregoric, cough medicines, toothpaste, and in most of the medicines and foods you think of as "licorice-flavored." It is thought to be good for indigestion and other stomach troubles and to ease coughing; licorice (anise-flavored) pastilles are sucked on by opera singers before a performance to soothe their throats.

Uses

Its culinary use ranges from breads, pastries, stews, candies, and pasta to anisette, a well-known French cordial. All of the plant can be used in salads, and the seeds can be eaten as a condiment.

If you buy anise, instead of growing it and drying it yourself, always buy it as seed rather than powdered. It is very delicate, and powdered anise will lose its flavor long before you have used up the jar. The seed keeps fairly well and can be ground with a mortar and pestle or with a Chinese cleaver if your recipes require ground anise.

When to Plant

Anise takes 120 days to reach maturity, so it should be planted as soon as the soil is thoroughly warmed and all danger of frost is past. Since seed can be harvested green, it need not reach full maturity in the garden. If you wish to get a jump on the season, start the seed indoors.

How to Plant

For starting seed indoors, use Cornell Mix (*see* Glossary) and a flat or similar container with good drainage. Sow seeds ¼ inch deep. Do not let the soil dry out; it should be moist but not wet. Cover lightly with plastic until the first green shoots appear; the plastic should be lifted and allowed to dry if moisture condenses on the side facing the soil.

Outdoors, sow ¼ inch deep, in rows 12 inches apart.

Thinning

Thin to 8″–12″ apart when the seedlings start to crowd one another. Use the thinnings minced in salads.

Culture

It is very important to keep anise evenly watered, but slightly on the dry side. If you're expecting a hot spell, water twenty-four hours before, if possible; in any case, do not alternately soak the soil and then let it dry out completely.

Harvest

If you want to gather leaves for salads, you can do this all summer long. Do not strip the plant—you will still want it to have strength enough to set seed—but a scattering of plants in your flower bed should give you enough fresh leaves for the season. A little minced anise leaf goes a long way.

The seed will ripen unevenly, so some will be ripe while others are still green. This would make harvesting difficult if it were not for the fact that the plant can be taken from the garden while some of the seeds are still green, stacked in tied bundles in a dry place, and allowed to ripen. Treated this way, the seeds will not shatter and can be gathered at your leisure.

Varieties

Herbs are not usually listed by varieties. The important thing is to be sure you are getting the correct herb (anise instead of cumin, for instance).

Most catalogs list anise, though you may have to look under "herbs" in the index rather than under "anise." Nichols, which specializes in herbs and rare seeds, does not have an index, and you will have to leaf through their tempting pages to locate what you want.

DILL
Anethum graveolens

A study of the culinary arts of ancient times always leaves me with a great admiration for the cooks and physicians of long ago. They knew almost all the herbs we use today, both their culinary and medicinal properties, and modern knowledge has added little to that of the past. Dill is an example of an herb of ancient use.

History

Native to southern Russia and the lands around the Mediterranean, dill is still found growing wild among the corn in Portugal and Spain, as well as along the coast in other Mediterranean countries. Today it is cultivated all over the world, although the largest crops come from India and Japan.

The Greeks and Romans used both dill leaves and seeds to flavor salads and cooked dishes, as well as medicinally as a cure for hiccups, as a carminative, and for inducing sleep; in fact, dill owes its name to a Norse word for "lull." It is mentioned in old herbals, and in the Middle Ages was considered an effective charm against witches.

Dill is used in medicine today for many of the same ailments as in olden times, and is still considered helpful in treating insomnia—although I would not suggest that the ingestion of several dill pickles just before bedtime would serve the purpose.

A few drops of oil of dill in water is a home remedy for stomach discomfort in children, and it is popular as a flavoring for children's medicines.

Uses

I have included dill among the few herbs I would suggest you grow in your salad garden for two reasons: it is very versatile, as both leaves and seeds are used; it is not truly appreciated in this country, and you will easily gain a reputation for your unusual dishes if you keep it handy on your spice shelf.

When to Plant

Dill is an easy-to-grow annual and should be planted as early in the spring as the ground can be worked, especially if you wish to produce seeds.

How to Plant

Dill, like fennel, is very attractive and would be pretty in the flower bed. However, it is also good in the vegetable garden where its feathery foliage is a pleasant contrast to coarser vegetable foliage. Dill plants grow 2′–4′ in height.

It does best in a sunny, well-drained location—against a fence is good, since the plants are sometimes spindly and a windy spot may cause them to become untidy-looking. You can always secure the row lightly to the fence with a soft cotton cord about two-thirds of the way up the full-grown plants; this will be sufficient to keep them from flopping over but will not be as much work as individual staking. Another way to grow them is among your early peas; they can be secured to the same support the peas use and will remain after the peas are harvested and removed.

Sow seeds $\frac{1}{4}$ inch deep 6″–8″ apart in rows 9 inches apart. Seeds germinate quickly and the plant grows rapidly. It is particularly helpful in the garden to have something growing briskly when all the other plants look as if they will never get beyond the seedling stage.

Culture

Dill isn't fussy. It prefers a light soil and should be fertilized at least once during the growing season. As with all vegetables, water regularly. If you mulch, as I think you always should, weeds won't be a problem. If you don't, I imagine you have your own way of dealing with the weeds.

Harvest

Here, as with fennel, when you harvest depends on what you harvest. The leaves can be taken anytime you need a few for your salads or cooking. Don't take too many from any one plant if you want a seed crop; don't take the top of the plant, or you will interfere with seed production. The best way is to use some plants for their leaves and keep some uncropped for maximum seed production. Since dill produces large quantities of seeds, this is not a hardship.

To harvest seeds, wait until they are ripe; ripe seeds look flat and brown. Dry them on flat trays, covering the seeds with a single layer of cheesecloth; they are so light the slightest breeze will scatter them.

If you wish to dry the foliage for winter use, cut the whole plant near the ground and hang up in a warm, dry place until the leaves crumble easily. Then either rub the leaves between the palms of your hands or put the whole plant into a paper bag, tie tightly at the top, and store in a warm, dry place.

By the way, if you want to save the seeds for future crops, it is comforting to know that they will stay viable for three years.

Varieties

Almost all seedsmen list dill. Look under "herbs" and don't worry about varieties. Dill is dill.

FLORENCE FENNEL
Foeniculum dulce

Many gardeners and cooks are not acquainted with Florence—
or sweet—fennel, an herb that has practically crossed the line
into vegetable. If you are ordering seeds, be sure you get this
kind and not the common or Italian fennel, which has a similar
flavor but does not form the thick white aboveground bulb.
Most catalogs are careful to identify it properly as Florence
fennel. Burpee says it has an "enlarged, flat-oval leaf base."
Thompson & Morgan says the "chunky base root looks like
celery." The descriptions are, on the whole, unsatisfactory—it is
certainly not a root—but will serve as a guide if you read carefully.

History

As far as we know, fennel originated around the Mediterranean shores; today it grows wild in many parts of the world,
from India to Wales. It is cultivated for export primarily in the
South of France, and in Russia, Iran, and India.

Common fennel was much loved by the Romans. Pliny
ascribed no less than twenty-two specific medicinal uses to it,
including giving strength and courage, increasing longevity, as
a carminative, and for strengthening eyesight.

Like dill, it was thought to be efficacious against witches and
the evil eye, and was hung over the front door on Midsummer
Eve for that purpose.

Charlemagne, that indefatigable gardener, included it on his
imperial farm, and herbalists everywhere grew it extensively.

Uses

Fennel has a delicious anise-like flavor. The leaves, stalks, and bulb are all edible. Chopped up in salads, braised or added to stews, used on top of charcoal for a superb grilled fish—all the uses of fennel are delectable. Once you have grown it in your garden and used it in your kitchen, you will wonder how you ever did without it.

When to Plant

Wait until the soil is thoroughly warm.

How to Plant

Sow thinly, cover with 1 inch fine soil, firm well, and water.

Fennel is very decorative; the feathery foliage looks much like dill. It is attractive in the flower bed as well as in the vegetable or herb garden. Plant it in rich soil if you want to be sure to form the bulb.

Culture

Thin to stand 8 inches apart; the plants will grow about 1′–3′ tall. Use the thinnings in salads or dry for future use.

Water well and frequently and keep mulched, so that the soil does not get too dried out. As the bulbs form, blanch them by covering with foil or paper, or draw up the earth around them.

Harvest

The foliage can be picked as soon as the plant is a foot tall; leave some to feed and nurture the plant—you will still have enough to mince for your salads.

When the bulb is mature—about a week or ten days after it starts to swell—pick the whole plant. Cut off the stalks and foliage and use fresh in cooking, or dry and store in tightly covered containers away from heat and sun. Use the stalks to stuff fish or poultry (to impart flavor, not to eat) or for charcoal cookery; use the foliage to eat in salads or sprinkled on cooked vegetables as you would do with parsley.

The bulbs can be stored in a cool place and will keep for some time if carefully wrapped in plastic so that they do not dry out.

Varieties

Most catalogs do not bother to list varieties, and some catalogs are confusing because they list Florence fennel, meaning the bulb kind, and sweet fennel, meaning the non-bulb variety. This is incorrect nomenclature, since Florence fennel and sweet fennel are the same. It is also sometimes called finocchio, which is correct.

If varieties are given, there is usually only one, so you won't have any trouble making a choice. Look for it under "herbs" in the catalog index.

PARSLEY
Petroselinum crispum

In some ways, parsley is so well known that it is not known at all. We take for granted the parsley garnish served up in restaurants with sandwiches, fish, salads, and lamb chops, and most Americans carefully put the brilliant green sprig to one side and go on with their dinner.

Recently, however, frequenters of certain hamburger joints have found heaping bowls of parsley on the counters along with the sliced onions, and have learned that chewing on a bit of parsley will cleanse all trace of onion from their breath. This works with garlic, too, so parsley should be well thought of as a sociable herb, since it helps to keep people companionable no matter what they eat.

History

Parsley is a member of the carrot family and so closely related to celery that its Latin name means "rock celery." It apparently originated in the lands around the Mediterranean but has adapted to many other climes, growing freely in England and throughout Europe, as well as in the United States.

The Greeks and Romans were well acquainted with its medicinal properties, many of which we esteem even today. It was used as garlands at Greek and Roman feasts to ward off drunkenness as well as to crown heroes. It was an herb beloved by Venus; by extension, it was also commonly said that newborn babies could be found in clumps of it.

Parsley is rich in iron as well as vitamins A, B, and C; it is also thought to be an aid to digestion, so the next time you find a few leaflets on your plate, take the hint and eat them.

Uses

Parsley can be eaten raw or cooked. It is an attractive and tasty garnish, as well as the main ingredient in a classic salad; it contributes zest and nutrients to stews and casseroles. Fried parsley is delicious if eaten immediately upon being prepared. Curly parsley is the type we use as a garnish; Italian parsley, with a stronger flavor and flatter leaf, is better for cooking.

When to Plant

Since parsley does very well indoors, you can plant it anytime you please. Outdoors, however, it may be planted as soon as the ground can be worked—and from then on until early August. If you want to pot plants, take them indoors before a heavy frost, although in a sheltered spot parsley may winter over. I have often gathered parsley from under the snow in the middle of December.

How to Plant

Planting parsley takes a combination of confidence and patience: confidence to believe that you really planted something; patience to wait until the seed germinates.

Parsley is so slow to germinate that old-time gardeners decided it was an herb that had to go down to the devil nine times for consultation before it could actually germinate. Allow two to four weeks; it may take even longer.

To plant, soak the seed in *very* warm water overnight and sow immediately the next morning, covering the seed with a bare ¼ inch of fine soil tamped down firmly. Plants should stand 3″–6″ apart, rows 12″–24″ apart.

Culture

Once it has germinated, parsley is trouble-free. It will grow well in a partly sunny spot and likes somewhat moist conditions, but it will tolerate a dry, sunny place if necessary. If the soil is slightly acid, add lime or wood ashes.

Although parsley is a biennial, it will go to seed the second year, so it is better sown each spring. Some gardeners have good luck with letting some of their plants go to seed and self-sow; since I want my parsley in certain places and not in others, I prefer to plant seeds each year. Once you resign yourself to the slow germination rate, parsley presents no problems.

Harvest

Gather it anytime—both to use and to dry. It keeps well in the refrigerator, grows happily on the windowsill, and can be frozen.

Varieties

Parsley is usually listed under its own name in seed catalog indexes, rather than just under "herbs." You will order by types rather than by varieties: CURLY PARSLEY is the frilly garnish type; ITALIAN, PLAIN, or SINGLE-LEAVED PARSLEY has a flat leaf and a better flavor—it is not suitable for garnishing.

Some catalogs also list PARSNIP-ROOTED, TURNIP-ROOTED, or HAMBURG PARSLEY; this is a root vegetable, a true parsley, but the roots rather than the leaves are eaten.

Do not be confused if you see a listing for CHINESE PARSLEY. This is the herb coriander. We are more familiar with the seeds than with the leaves, but in Chinese cooking the leaves are used; they have a very special aroma and taste and, if used with discretion, add an interesting difference to familiar dishes. Coriander seeds don't taste anything like the fresh leaves and cannot be substituted successfully for them in recipes.

I have heard there is another kind of parsley grown in Finland, but none of the catalogs lists it and I have never grown it.

GARDENER INTO GOURMET

And by now—if you have been faithfully following the directions in all these chapters—you are practically munching on your first radishes, so off we go to the kitchen.

PART II

THE SALAD
KITCHEN

CHAPTER SEVEN

Entertaining Salads

ALL OF THESE SALADS can be served as part of a meal. Many of them make an excellent luncheon main dish or a tasty side dish. I have gathered them together here for party occasions. Salads are so easy to entertain with—easy on the hostess, who can do much of the preparation ahead of time, and easy on the budget, because the interest lies in a subtle blending of flavor, texture, and color rather than in the most expensive cut of meat.

The exception to this, of course, is my first recipe, but I could not resist one really luxurious note in an otherwise mostly realistic culinary world.

CAVIAR

If you ever have an occasion so special or a budget so generous that you want to serve caviar, here is how it is traditionally done.

Only a fine crystal bowl will do as a container—even if you have to borrow it. Chill the bowl in the refrigerator, then set in a bed of crushed ice. Spoon in the caviar and put a small silver spoon on one side for serving.

Surround with small crystal dishes of fine-chopped onion, wedges of fresh lemon, fine-chopped hard-cooked egg yolk, fine-chopped hard-cooked egg white, and plates of thin homemade toast. Guests should be allowed to help themselves and choose their own garnishes.

Champagne is, of course, the preferred beverage.

Note: Customarily, only black caviar receives this treatment, but since red caviar has become so expensive, I don't see why you couldn't serve it the same way. The only change I would make is to add a bowl of sour cream.

SMORGASBORD

A smorgasbord is much more fun than a cocktail party. It is meant to accompany liquor but an invitation to a smorgasbord is different from a cocktail party because the food is more of a meal. Around holiday time—or any time of year—you can return many social obligations with this happy combination of cocktail party and buffet supper.

Traditionally, a smorgasbord includes both hot and cold dishes; the hot dishes can be simply taken care of with pyttipanna (see *Summer Garden, Winter Kitchen* for this recipe), tiny boiled new potatoes garnished with minced dill, Boston baked beans, and a simple fish custard.

Recipes for the cold salads are given on the following pages.

Your smorgasbord table could include the following:

> Pyttipanna
> Boiled new potatoes with dill

Boston baked beans
Fish custard
Herring salad
Beets Tivoli
Veal in aspic
Anchovy eggs
Stuffed mushrooms
Boiled ham platter
Celery and carrot sticks
Tossed green salad
Cheese platter
Suitable breads and crispbreads
Danish pastry
Coffee

HERRING SALAD

It is perfectly proper to serve assorted kinds of imported Scandi-navian herrings right in their tins. However, if you wish to pre-pare something special, this could be it.

SERVES 6–8

2 large pickled herrings
4 cups boiled potatoes, diced
1 cup celeriac, diced
1/3 cup mixed sweet pickles, diced
2 cups pickled beets, diced
1/2 cup scallions, sliced thin
1 cup apples, not peeled, diced
1/4 cup cider vinegar
1 1/2 tablespoons sugar
1 1/2 tablespoons water
1/2 tablespoon dill
Salt and pepper, to taste

Remove all bones from herring and chop into bite-sized pieces (on the small side).

Combine all ingredients and toss gently but mix thoroughly. Let stand in refrigerator overnight.

Serving suggestions: Serve in bowl with garnish of curly parsley sprigs or hard-cooked egg wedges, or accompany with a dish of sour cream.

BEETS TIVOLI

SERVES 4

½ cup brown sugar
½ cup water
½ cup cider vinegar
1 clove garlic, minced
1 teaspoon salt
¼ teaspoon pepper
2 cups cooked beets, sliced thin

In saucepan heat sugar, water, vinegar, garlic, salt, and pepper to boiling point. Boil just 2 minutes.

Place beets in glass dish and cover with hot vinegar mixture. Cool slowly. Cover and refrigerate overnight. If liquid doesn't cover beets, turn them gently every so often to keep moist.

Drain and serve.

VEAL IN ASPIC

This is so easy it's almost sinful.

SERVES 6–8

4 pounds of veal for stew (boneless), cut into 1½-inch cubes
1 tablespoon thyme
½ teaspoon basil

2 garlic cloves, minced
1/4 cup lemon juice
1 tablespoon dry mustard
1/2 cup chives
Salt and pepper, to taste
Carrot, grated

Combine all ingredients, except carrot, in a suitably sized saucepan and cover with cold water.

Bring to a boil and turn down to simmer. Do not allow to boil even if you have to put it on another burner.

Simmer gently for 2 hours. Put into serving dish—it could be two large lasagne pans, for instance—and chill overnight. Stir when it is convenient, to distribute the meat throughout the liquid.

The next day the mixture will have turned into a jelly. Cut it into wedges (but do not remove from the dish) and serve garnished with grated carrot in interesting patterns. Guests can help themselves with a small spatula or knife.

ANCHOVY EGGS

SERVES 12

1 dozen hard-cooked eggs
1/2 cup mayonnaise
1 can anchovies, minced (not drained)
2 tablespoons lemon juice
1/4 teaspoon dry mustard
3 tablespoons butter
Salt, if needed

Cut eggs in half. Remove yolks carefully without breaking the whites.

Set the whites aside. Combine the yolks with all the remaining ingredients and mash until smooth. Beat lightly with fork or small whisk to make slightly fluffy, or put through pastry tube. Fill reserved egg whites with mixture. Chill at least 1 hour.

Serving suggestion: Arrange on platter decorated with tomato wedges and pimiento flowers.

STUFFED MUSHROOMS

3 pounds large mushrooms
3 tubes shrimp paste
1 stick butter
1 cup sour cream
3 tablespoons dill
Parsley, for garnish

Do not peel mushrooms if they are fresh. Wipe with damp paper towel or cloth and take off stems. With spoon, gently scoop out enough of underside of mushroom caps to make a secure hole.

Mince scooped-out mushroom bits and mash by hand with all other ingredients except parsley. Fill mushroom caps with mixture. Sprinkle with parsley.

Arrange on platter with curly parsley sprigs.

Note: The mushroom stems can be sliced, marinated in pickle juice with a clove of crushed garlic, and served as a separate dish.

THE SALAD BAR

A fairly recent American innovation is the salad bar. The best—as well as the most modest—restaurants feature it as a special attraction, and people who always thought of salads as "rabbit food" are happily and trustfully heaping their plates with greens and a variety of ingredients from sometimes mysterious-looking bowls. Everyone seems to enjoy salad bars, and there is no doubt they have saved many a dull meal.

What most hostesses do not realize, however, is that a salad bar can serve as an easy buffet. The well-planned salad bar is very attractive to look at and gives you a chance to show off all your odd pieces of china, pottery, or crystal. It is easy to prepare days ahead of your party, and it is economical because almost all the ingredients that remain uneaten are unspoiled and can be used in many new ways on subsequent days—not just as leftovers.

The difference between the salad bar that serves as a buffet for a party and the salad bar in a restaurant is that the home salad bar should be a complete main course in itself. This means it needs to be more substantial, and should include protein such as meat, eggs, or cheese in sufficient quantity to give a satisfied feeling. If you think you need something still more substantial, simply add a roast such as turkey or ham—or a bowl of shrimp. The salad bar should always include an interesting selection of breads—great round loaves of Italian bread sliced so they still show their shape, small pretty loaves of quick breads such as parsnip bread, carrot bread, and other vegetable non-sweet breads. There should also be butter in balls or pats, something manageable for the guest serving himself.

Needless to say, many guests will carry over their drinks, but liquid refreshment such as an inexpensive chilled wine, pitchers of your own recipe of sangría, of beer, and of soft drinks should be on hand.

Dessert can be any of your usual favorites. Something as simple as a choice of cookies or cheesecake will go very well. Rich desserts are not usually desirable after a meal of salad, but you can always serve one really luscious cake if you want to.

Hot coffee and tea will be welcome—in addition, Irish coffee makes a really grand finale.

The following salad bars are just a few of my favorite combinations. I am sure your own imagination will suggest many, many more.

Summer Salad Bar

The basis of the salad is, of course, the greens—but the excitement and adventure lie in the bowls of things to add and in interesting dressings. Quantities are not indicated, because only you know the size of your party; you can always have some extra in reserve in case your buffet is too great a success.

Large bowls (at least 2) of crisp, well-washed, bite-sized, and well-mixed:

> Romaine lettuce
> Watercress
> Salad Bowl lettuce

Medium-sized bowls of each of the following:

> Red onions, sliced and separated into rings
> Cherry tomatoes
> Yellow plum tomatoes, halved
> Zucchini, diced
> Red and green peppers, diced
> Curly parsley sprigs
> Hard-cooked eggs, minced

Red radishes, sliced
Ham and turkey, julienne
Parmesan cheese, grated
Croutons

Bowls, with small ladles, of salad dressings:

Russian dressing
Roquefort dressing (see recipe page 169)
Aïoli (see recipe page 175)
Cruets of olive oil and vinegar

Winter Salad Bar

Large bowls of well-washed, dried, crisped, and bite-sized:

Young beet greens
Chinese cabbage
Celery tops
Spinach
Iceberg lettuce (not too much of this)

Medium-sized bowls of each of the following:

Jerusalem artichokes, diced (keep in
    lemon water, with slotted serving
    spoon)
Chickpeas
Bacon, broiled and crumbled
Shallots, minced with grated carrots
Cooked beets, sliced
Onion rings
Mushrooms, sliced
Boiled chicken, julienne

        Cooked peas (not canned)
        Croutons
        Tomatoes, sliced
        Pitted black olives
        Hot Italian sausage, cooked and crumbled

Small bowls of:

        Roquefort cheese, crumbled
        Parmesan cheese, grated
        Peanuts, chopped
        Dill, minced

Bowls, with small ladles, of salad dressings:

        Curried mayonnaise, thinned with cream
        Green Goddess dressing (see recipe page 165)
        Cruets of garlic olive oil and wine vinegar

Basque Salad Bar

Large bowls of well-washed, dried, crisped, and bite-sized:

        Ruby lettuce

Medium-sized bowls of each of the following:

Cucumbers, sliced
Onions, sliced
Cooked baby lima beans mixed with pimientos
Pitted green olives, sliced, mixed with sliced marinated carrots
Hard-cooked eggs, sliced
Skinless and boneless sardines, halved
Cooked shrimp, halved (unless tiny)

Tuna fish, flaked
Italian parsley, chopped
Boiled potatoes, diced large

Small bowls of:

> Mozzarella cheese, cubed
> Fresh basil, minced
> Curly parsley sprigs

Bowls, with small ladles, of salad dressings:

> Herbed mayonnaise, thinned with heavy cream
> Russian dressing
> Cruets of olive oil and tarragon vinegar

HORS D'OEUVRES

If you have a small congenial group, you may choose to serve a very simple dinner—say, lemon chicken, a good tossed salad, and an interesting rice dish. In this case, it might be nice to break with tradition and skip cocktails or limit them to just one. Serve wine instead at the table, with several dishes of delectable hors d'oeuvres with French bread and sweet butter. Be sure to allow for plenty of wine, though, or the party may never get off its feet.

STUFFED CELERY

> 12 celery stalks, washed and cut into 4-inch lengths
> 8-ounce package cream cheese
> 1/4 pound Roquefort cheese, crumbled
> 1 garlic clove, minced
> 2 tablespoons chives, minced

Crisp celery by standing in ice water for ½ hour. Blend all remaining ingredients except for chives. Fill celery stalks with blended mixture squeezed through a pastry tube, and sprinkle with chives. Chill in refrigerator until time to serve.

MUSHROOM EGGS

4 hard-cooked eggs
2 cups pickled beets, minced
3 tablespoons sour cream
1 tablespoon turmeric
Salt and pepper, to taste
Carrot, grated

Cut eggs in half. Remove yolks carefully without breaking whites.

Set whites aside. Combine the yolks with all the remaining ingredients, except carrot, and mash together. Stuff reserved egg whites with mixture and garnish with carrot.

VEGETABLE SAVORY

4 shallots, minced
2 scallions, sliced thin
½ cup Spanish onion, chopped
3 tablespoons olive oil
3 tomatoes, chopped
3 eggplants, diced
8 pitted black olives, sliced
2 tablespoons lemon juice

Sauté shallots, scallions, and onions in olive oil until lightly golden and soft. Add remaining ingredients, stir to blend well, cover and cook about 10 minutes, or until soft.

Chill before serving. Will keep for several days in the refrigerator.

YOGURT CHEESE CUBES

1 quart plain yogurt
3 tablespoons anise, powdered
Salt, to taste
3 cups walnuts, chopped

Line colander or sieve with 3 thicknesses of clean cheesecloth. Blend yogurt with anise and salt, and pour into cheesecloth. Pull ends of cheesecloth together and tie. Do this around noon and allow to drain overnight.

In the morning, the cheese should be formed and firm enough to cut into cubes. The first time you try the recipe, do it a couple of days ahead so you see how it works for you; the cheese will keep that long in cold water in the refrigerator if you change the water once a day.

Heap on serving plate and sprinkle generously with walnuts.

Note: If the cheese isn't firm enough to cube, pack into an attractive small dish and serve with a spreader.

STUFFED ARTICHOKE HEARTS

1 package frozen artichoke hearts
¼ cup lemon juice
1½ cups guacamole (see recipe page 159)
Lemon wedges

Cook artichokes according to directions on package. Toss with lemon juice.

When cool enough to handle, scoop out a little of the center to make a hole—an iced-tea spoon works well for this. Mince centers you have removed and reserve.

Chill. Meanwhile make guacamole. Be sure artichokes are liberally sprinkled with lemon juice so they do not discolor. When thoroughly chilled, mix guacamole with reserved minced artichoke bits and stuff the hearts. Garnish with lemon wedges.

CHAPTER EIGHT

Tossed Salads

HERE ARE SALADS to serve as a main dish or as a side dish at dinner, luncheon, or supper. It is impossible to give exact quantities because how much salad any one person will eat is a complete unknown. I have been at dinners where the entire salad bowl would have made one side portion for any member of my family. In any case, it is perfectly good form to run out of salad—so long as it is not the main course. If it is the main course, make more than you think you need and refrigerate it in a plastic bag; just do not put the dressing on it and you will be able to use it for a week.

RICE BOWL SALAD

SERVES 6

2 green peppers, blanched and cooled
2 cups rice, cooked

6 tomatoes, in chunks
1 onion, minced
1 garlic clove, minced
3 hard-cooked eggs, chopped
2 tablespoons Italian parsley, chopped
1 teaspoon turmeric
Salt and pepper, to taste
½ cup olive oil
¼ cup tarragon vinegar

Cut peppers in thin strips. Combine with all other ingredients, except seasonings, oil, and vinegar. Chill thoroughly.

Just before serving, stir seasonings into oil and pour over salad. Add vinegar. Toss to blend.

Note: When tossing a salad with oil and vinegar, add the oil first and toss to coat the greens thoroughly before adding vinegar.

SALAD CHINOISE

SERVES 8

¾ pound bean sprouts (mixed, if you grow your own)
4 scallions, sliced thin
5 red radishes, sliced thin
2 white radishes, sliced thin
2 cups raw broccoli florets, halved
½ cup peanuts, chopped
1 head Oak Leaf lettuce, washed, dried, and bite-sized
2 tablespoons sesame seeds

DRESSING: 2 tablespoons peanut oil
1 tablespoon sesame oil

2 tablespoons cider vinegar
1 tablespoon rice vinegar
1 tablespoon soy sauce
½ teaspoon fresh ginger, grated

Blend dressing ingredients thoroughly. Combine salad ingredients and toss gently with dressing.

TABBOULEH

Bulgur is a grain used widely in the Middle East. It is very nourishing, with an unusual nutty flavor. Almost every supermarket carries it, sometimes in the gourmet food section. This dish is easily a meal in itself.

SERVES 6–8

6 bunches Italian parsley, chopped
4 bunches curly parsley, chopped
1 bunch Chinese parsley, chopped
4 cups cooked bulgur, cooled
3 bunches scallions, sliced thin
6 tomatoes, chopped
¾ cup lemon juice
½ cup orange juice
3 tablespoons olive oil
1 tablespoon sesame oil
¼ cup toasted sesame seeds

Combine all ingredients except sesame seeds. Chill briefly. Sprinkle with sesame seeds just before serving.

CHEF'S SALAD

This is probably the most popular salad with men. However, it is often given little extra touches which are really unnecessary to the almost perfect combination of textures and flavors that have made it such a favorite. Be as original as you like with other salads, but stick to the classic recipe when serving this one. It is, of course, a meal in itself.

SERVES 6

> 1½ heads lettuce (see below)
> ½ pound roast turkey, white meat only, julienne
> ½ pound boiled ham, julienne
> ½ pound imported Swiss cheese, julienne
> Parsley, for garnish (optional)
> Vinaigrette dressing No. 1 (see recipe page 173)

The choice of lettuce is usually iceberg type in the United States, but here I depart from tradition and prefer a head of Salad Bowl with ½ head of romaine for crispness.

A large bowl should be filled with the salad greens and the rest of the ingredients laid on top, in the center, in the following order: first turkey, then ham, then Swiss cheese. The cheese may be garnished with a little minced parsley.

The vinaigrette dressing—or whatever you prefer—should be served separately; add to the salad and toss at the table.

MIXED GREEN SALAD

In a way, this is the true test of a salad maker. Unless your greens are fresh, washed, properly dried, torn—never cut—into bite-sized pieces and served with a zippy dressing, you will have a very dull dish. But made right, there is no salad more superb than this simple combination of greens.

SERVES 8

½ head Buttercrunch lettuce
½ head escarole

½ head chicory (heart and the more tender of the outer leaves)
¼ head Salad Bowl

Separate leaves, discard any that are not perfect. Wash in colander under cold running water. None of these greens should be sandy, but if by some chance they are, soak separately for 5 minutes in lukewarm water, then rinse and crisp in cold water.

Drain, dry, and put in a bowl lined with 4 thicknesses of paper toweling. Chill in refrigerator. Bring greens and dressing to the table separately. Combine and toss just before serving.

I would suggest only 2 dressings for this salad: vinaigrette No. 1 or Green Goddess (see recipes pages 165 and 173).

CAESAR SALAD

This is one you won't find in old cookbooks, but it has become a true classic and a great favorite.

SERVES 6

2 cups stale bread, cubed
2 cloves garlic, minced
3 tablespoons olive oil
2 romaine lettuces, washed, dried, and chilled
1 whole raw egg
2 tablespoons lemon juice
Salt and pepper, to taste
½ cup Parmesan cheese, grated fresh

Brown cubed bread croutons with minced garlic in hot olive oil until golden on all sides. Remove bread from oil with slotted spoon and put on paper toweling to drain, turning occasionally. This can be done the day before and the croutons kept crisp in a plastic bag. Let olive oil cool and reserve.

Break romaine into manageable pieces—not too small makes a better-looking salad. Pour cool olive oil over romaine and toss until greens are completely coated and minced garlic is distributed throughout the salad.

Combine egg, lemon juice, salt, and pepper, and beat slightly. Add to greens and toss. Add cheese and toss. Add croutons, toss quickly, and serve while the croutons are still crisp.

Note: If you don't want to serve actual garlic, crush 2 garlic cloves and put in olive oil the day before. Remove cloves and use oil without garlic. Most Caesar salad recipes include anchovies as an optional ingredient. I love anchovies but in this case I think they overpower the unusual combination of other flavors.

SHRIMP SALAD

SERVES 8

3 cups whole cooked shrimp
2 cups whole pitted black olives
3 onions, sliced and separated into rings
4 hard-cooked eggs, chopped
1 cup anchovies, chopped
2 bunches watercress, in 2-inch pieces
1 head romaine, torn in bite-sized pieces
1 cup aïoli dressing (see recipe page 175), thinned with heavy
   cream

If the shrimp are very large, cut into medium-sized pieces; the important thing is that the eater get a good chunk of shrimp when he takes a bite. If you prefer, you can substitute lobster or crabmeat, or use a combination of all three. Just remember to keep the pieces man-sized.

Combine all ingredients except dressing. Toss with dressing and serve.

CHAPTER NINE

Salad Plates

HERE ARE SALADS that can be served with the meat course or as a separate course at the beginning of a meal. Although I usually suggest a dressing for them, you may serve a choice (not more than two) at the table or substitute an entirely different one. Sauces and dressings for salads depend on what else is to be eaten with them. A heavy main course goes best with a light vinaigrette; a light main course can be offset with a richer dressing. In any case, mood, time of year, and menu are all variables, and you should feel free to deviate from recommendations that are purely arbitrary on my part.

JAPANESE CUCUMBER SALAD

SERVES 6–8

2 cucumbers, peeled
½ cup water

½ cup cider vinegar
½ teaspoon sugar
¼ teaspoon salt

Slice cucumbers paper-thin. Combine all other ingredients and pour over cucumbers. Chill in refrigerator ½ hour, drain, and serve as a side dish.

Serving suggestion: This should be served on small plates—like bread-and-butter plates or Japanese dishes made for salads —and garnished with very fresh, tiny red radishes (not more than 1 or 2 per serving) , a few julienne of celeriac, and 1 or 2 tiny shrimp.

ENDIVE SALAD

SERVES 6

6 Belgian endives
Walnut sauce (see recipe page 170)

Remove any imperfect leaves, cut a thin slice off the bottom of each endive, and cut endive in half lengthwise. Rinse in cold water to make sure there is no sand or earth between the outer leaves, but keep halves intact.

Place 2 halves on each salad plate and spoon walnut sauce over them. Serve immediately.

To Keep Green Peas Till Christmas

Take young peas, shell them, put them in a cullender to drain, then lay a cloth four or five times double on a table, then spread them on, dry them very well, and have your bottles ready, fill them, cover them with mutton suet fat when it is a little soft; fill the necks almost to the top, cork them, tie a bladder and a leather over them and let them stay in a dry cool place.

Recipe from an eighteenth-century American cookbook.

FRUIT SALAD

On each salad plate arrange:

Buttercrunch lettuce or similar greens
4 orange slices
4 onion slices, separated into rings
4 grapefruit segments, preferably pink
4 melon balls, cantaloupe and honeydew or watermelon
4 seedless grapes
1 tablespoon cottage cheese

Serving suggestions: Serve with sour cream fruit dressing (see recipe page 170) or pineapple mayonnaise (page 173), thinned with cream.

CRUNCHY SALAD

A welcome mixture of texture and color.

SERVES 6

3 McIntosh apples
1 tablespoon lemon juice
3 cups celeriac, blanched and diced
1 cup raw peanuts, coarsely chopped
¾ cup mayonnaise
¼ cup sour cream
Salt and pepper, to taste

6 lettuce cups
1 tablespoon parsley, minced
1 teaspoon chervil, minced

Core and chop apples, but do not peel. Use really red ones if possible. Toss with lemon juice.

Add celeriac and peanuts.

Combine mayonnaise, sour cream, salt, and pepper. Add to salad and mix well. Spoon into lettuce cups. Sprinkle with parsley and chervil.

SULTANA ORANGE SALAD

SERVES 6

1 cup sultana raisins
1/4 cup triple sec
1 cup yogurt
2 tablespoons mayonnaise
1 tablespoon fresh lemon juice
1/4 teaspoon cardamom
Salt and pepper, to taste
6 navel oranges, peeled and sliced
1 head Bibb lettuce, washed and dried

Soak raisins in triple sec for 1 hour. Blend yogurt and mayonnaise and add raisins and triple sec, lemon juice, cardamom, salt, and pepper.

Arrange orange slices over lettuce leaves spread on individual salad plates. When ready to serve, pour dressing generously over oranges.

HERBED GREEN BEANS

SERVES 4–6

1 pound Frenched green beans, cooked crisp
1/4 teaspoon fresh tarragon, minced
1/4 teaspoon shallots, minced
1 tablespoon olive oil
1 tablespoon wine vinegar
Salt and pepper, to taste

Combine all ingredients and chill for at least 1 hour.

Serving suggestions: Serve plain, or on individual plates over Belgian endive cut in 2-inch pieces and separated into leaves.

STUFFED CUCUMBERS

SERVES 6–8 AS A SALAD

3 cucumbers
3-ounce package cream cheese
1 tablespoon heavy cream
3 tablespoons shrimp paste
2 tablespoons onion, minced
2 tablespoons green pepper, minced
1 tablespoon fresh horseradish, grated
1 teaspoon lemon juice
1/2 teaspoon dill, minced
Salt and pepper, to taste
1 cup cooked brown rice

Peel cucumbers, hollow out by cutting off the ends and removing seeds with a zucchini corer or iced-tea spoon (a zucchini corer is much easier and quicker), and set aside.

Combine all other ingredients, except rice, and mash together until thoroughly blended. Mix in rice.

Stuff hollowed cucumbers with mixture and chill several hours or overnight.

Serving suggestions: To serve as canapés, slice stuffed cucumbers thin crosswise and put 1 slice each on Melba toast rounds. Dust lightly with paprika. To serve as salad, slice about ¼ inch thick, and lay several slices on a plate of lettuce leaves. Top each serving with a spoonful of mayonnaise garnished with chives.

MEDITERRANEAN CARROT SALAD

SERVES 8

2 pounds carrots, sliced
2 garlic cloves, crushed
¼ teaspoon turmeric
3 tablespoons vinegar
¼ teaspoon curry
¼ teaspoon cumin
½ tablespoon sugar
Salt and pepper, to taste
Iceberg lettuce, shredded

Combine all ingredients, except lettuce, and add enough water so that carrots are covered. Stir to mix.

Heat to simmering and continue to simmer, covered, for 10 minutes.

Refrigerate carrots in their liquid in covered jar for at least 2 days. Drain and serve on lettuce, dribbling some of the marinade over all.

MIMOSA SALAD

This salad classic takes its name from the garnish of hard-cooked eggs. A contrast in color is part of the charm of its appearance, so I prefer to make it with spinach, although other greens are acceptable.

SERVES 6–8

2 hard-cooked eggs
4–5 cups young spinach leaves, torn into bite-sized pieces

Separate the egg yolks from the whites. Chop the whites and crumble the yolks.

DRESSING : 2 tablespoons lemon juice
2 tablespoons olive oil
¼ tablespoon dry mustard
Salt and pepper, to taste

Combine all dressing ingredients in a covered jar and shake vigorously.

Put spinach in salad bowl, add dressing, and toss until well coated. Sprinkle egg whites in a flat round area in the center of the bowl. Sprinkle the crumbled yolks on top of the whites, leaving an outside ring of whites around the yolks.

Serve immediately or the salad will wilt.

SUNSHINE SALAD

Arrange on each salad plate:

4 yellow tomato slices
6 Lemon Cucumber slices
2 tablespoons raw carrot, grated

2 tablespoons raw yellow turnip, grated
Parsley, for garnish

Spoon over each plate mayonnaise thinned with cream and blended with enough saffron to color lightly. Garnish with minced curly parsley.

STUFFED AVOCADO
SERVES 2 AS AN APPETIZER OR SIDE DISH, 1 AS A MAIN COURSE

1 avocado
1 tablespoon lemon juice
½ cup boiled ham, minced
1 tablespoon Roquefort cheese, crumbled
1 black olive, minced
2 tablespoons yogurt
Salt and pepper, to taste
Dill, for garnish

Cut avocado in half, leaving shell on. Remove pit. Sprinkle avocado halves with lemon juice.

Combine all other ingredients except dill. Spoon into avocado halves. Garnish with fresh dill, minced.

Serving suggestion: Surround with a few frilly leaves of chicory.

PEAR SALAD
SERVES 2 AS AN APPETIZER OR SIDE DISH, 1 AS A MAIN COURSE

3-ounce package of cream cheese
1 teaspoon chives, chopped

1 teaspoon parsley, chopped
1 tablespoon crushed unsweetened pineapple, well drained
1 tablespoon sour cream
1 tablespoon unsweetened pineapple juice
Salt and pepper, to taste
1 pear
Toasted sesame seeds
Chinese cabbage, shredded

Blend together all ingredients except pear, sesame seeds, and cabbage. If the mixture is too stiff, add a little more pineapple juice.

Halve and seed pear. Fill with cream cheese mixture and sprinkle with sesame seeds. Serve on bed of Chinese cabbage.

Parsley, good in soups, and to garnish roast Beef, excellent with bread and butter in the spring.
From an eighteenth-century American cookbook.

FENNEL SALAD

SERVES 8

4 fennel bulbs
Chicory
Vinaigrette No. 1 (see recipe page 173)
Salt and pepper, to taste

Slice fennel lengthwise as thin as possible. Divide into 8 portions and lay slices on bed of chicory. The fennel, when sliced this way, has a very attractive pattern. Drizzle with dressing and season to taste.

To Make a Salad

*Let the herby ingredients be exquisitely cull'd and
cleans'd of all worm-eaten, dry-spotted leaves. Then
discreetly sprinkled with spring water. Let remain for
a while in a cullender, then swing gently in a clean
napkin.*

From *Acetaria, John Evelyn* (1620–1706).

CURRANT SALAD

SERVES 6

¼ cup dried currants
2 tablespoons sherry
2 cucumbers, sliced but not peeled (if unwaxed)
2 radishes, grated
2 carrots, grated
½ cup peanuts, chopped
1 teaspoon fresh mint, chopped
½ cup shallots, minced
Salt and pepper, to taste
1 head leaf lettuce

Soak currants in sherry overnight. Discard sherry or save for
another use.

Combine all ingredients except lettuce. Spoon onto lettuce
arranged on salad plates.

EARLY GARDEN SALAD

*This is in honor of the early vegetables, and everything should
be young and tender.*

SERVES 6–8

1 pound Swiss chard leaves
6 baby carrots, sliced

1 pound new potatoes, cooked and sliced

2 cups fresh green peas

2/3 cup mayonnaise, thinned with garlic vinegar

On each salad plate arrange Swiss chard leaves torn to bite size. Only the tiny, tender new leaves should be used. If you have Ruby chard, use that instead.

Combine carrots, potatoes, and peas, and spoon over Swiss chard. Top with mayonnaise.

CHICKEN SALAD DELHI

SERVES 8

2 cups mayonnaise

1 1/2 teaspoons curry powder

2 slices fresh ginger, minced

1 teaspoon cayenne

1/4 teaspoon cumin

Salt, if necessary

6 cups boiled chicken, cut in chunks

2 cups celery, chopped

1/2 cup pimientos, slivered

1 cup scallions, sliced thin

2 cups peas, cooked five minutes

3 cups cooked elbow macaroni

Romaine lettuce

Parsley

Combine mayonnaise with seasonings. Taste for salt and add if necessary.

Combine all other ingredients, except romaine and parsley, and stir in seasoned mayonnaise. Arrange romaine on individual salad plates and spoon mixture over it. Garnish with parsley **sprigs.**

CHAPTER TEN

Salads for All Seasons

THIS CHAPTER is a catchall for the many delectable recipes that I really did not want to put under any special category. Some, like the potato salad recipes, are equally good for picnics, Saturday night suppers or New Year's Day open house; others are little dishes of delightful flavors to refresh the appetite and add zest to a simple—even solitary—meal.

Browse through whenever you are looking for that one extra dish to complete a menu; or when imagination wavers and your own culinary repertoire seems suddenly too familiar.

LEMONY STUFFED GRAPE LEAVES

If you want to make a meal of these, you can add 3 cups chopped meat to the stuffing, but these are just as tasty and much less filling.

SERVES 8

16-ounce jar grape leaves
1 cup cooked rice
2 onions, chopped
3 tablespoons pine nuts, chopped
3 tablespoons parsley, minced (preferably Italian)
3 tablespoons mint leaves, minced
¼ teaspoon cardamom
¼ teaspoon anise
Salt and pepper, to taste
⅓ cup lemon juice
½ cup olive oil
2 cups chicken broth
1 garlic clove, crushed

The grape leaves will come in brine and must be rinsed in cold water, then in hot, to remove excess salt. The best way to do this is to place them in a large bowl, cover with cold water, drain in a colander. Then repeat with boiling water. Work quickly so the leaves do not cook and get too limp to handle.

While the leaves are cooling, combine rice, onions, pine nuts, parsley, mint, cardamom, anise, salt, and pepper to make the stuffing.

Stuff as you would cabbage leaves: place a small spoonful of stuffing near the stem end, then roll the leaf tightly, tucking in the sides as you go. As you roll the leaves, place them in a large pot lined with unrolled grape leaves (to keep the stuffed ones from possible scorching).

Once all the leaves have been stuffed and placed in the pot, combine the remaining ingredients and pour over the stuffed grape leaves.

Cover pot tightly, bring to a boil, and simmer for about an hour. Check occasionally—it may be necessary to add more broth or a little water.

SCANDINAVIAN SCRAMBLED EGGS

I first tasted this many years ago in a Danish restaurant, and I couldn't believe it. Now that I've learned more about the cuisines of other countries, I don't find the idea of cold scrambled eggs quite so unusual.

SERVES 3

1½ tablespoons butter
1 tablespoon shallots, minced
6 eggs, lightly beaten
1 tablespoon heavy cream
Salt and pepper, to taste
Curly parsley, for garnish

Heat butter in skillet until foam starts to subside. Sauté shallots until golden.

Combine eggs and cream. DO NOT ADD SALT AT THIS TIME. Pour into shallot-butter mixture and scramble quickly. If you usually make your scrambled eggs creamy, cook these a little longer, until slightly dry.

Toss with salt and pepper and allow to cool. Serve chilled or at room temperature, garnished with minced curly parsley.

HOW TO TELL IF EGGS ARE FRESH

The best possible method of ascertaining, is to put them into water, if they lye on their bilge, they are good and fresh—if they bob up on end, they are stale, and if these rise they are addled, proved and of no use.

From an eighteenth-century American cookbook.

COUNT RUMFORD'S POTATO SALAD

A dish in high repute in some parts of Germany, and which deserves to be particularly recommended, is a salad of potatoes. The potatoes being properly boiled and skinned are cut into thin slices, and the same sauce which is commonly used for salads of lettuce is poured over them. Some mix anchovies with this sauce, which gives it a very agreeable relish, and with potatoes it is remarkably palatable.

From *Receipts for Preparing Various Kinds of . . . Food . . . of Potatoes . . .* Collected Works of Count Rumford, Benjamin Thompson (1753–1814)

Tip: If a tossed salad is to be the main dish, be sure it includes protein—meat, fish, eggs, or beans. If it is to be an accompaniment to a meal, it can be as simple as mixed greens.

CRUDITES

This is the term used to describe bowls and plates of fresh, crisp raw vegetables served with a spicy dip. Guests choose whatever they want and dip the vegetables themselves. Crudités are very popular and more refreshing than most cocktail party fare. Here is a suggested combination—really limited only by your own imagination.

Carrot sticks
Celery sticks
Cucumber sticks

Turnip sticks
Fennel sticks
Broccoli florets
Cauliflower florets
Zucchini sticks
Beet sticks
Tiny Brussels sprouts, with toothpicks
Small red and yellow radishes, with toothpicks
Parsley or dill, for garnish

For dip, choose one of the spicy varieties, such as aïoli, Green Goddess with 1/4 teaspoon of cayenne added, or tahini (see recipes pages 165, 168, and 175). If too loose for a dip (as they tend to be), thicken with mayonnaise or sour cream, and correct seasoning to taste.

The secret of success in this dish is the perfection of the vegetables and their attractive arrangement. They can be garnished with curly parsley, dill, or fennel feathers if desired.

EGGPLANT SALAD

3 onions, chopped
3 garlic cloves, minced
1/2 cup olive oil
1 eggplant, diced but not peeled
4 small zucchini, diced
6 tomatoes, cut into eighths
1 tablespoon soy sauce

Sauté onions and garlic in olive oil. Add eggplant and zucchini and sauté, uncovered, 10 minutes. Add tomatoes and soy sauce. Stir to mix thoroughly. Cover and simmer 10 minutes. Chill and serve.

COOKED SPINACH SALAD

SERVES 6

4 cups cooked spinach, cooled
4 cups yogurt
1 teaspoon nutmeg
Salt and pepper, to taste
Rutabaga, grated

Combine all ingredients except rutabaga. Place in bowl and sprinkle with grated rutabaga.

HOT GERMAN POTATO SALAD
If any is left over, this is equally delicious cold.

6 potatoes
¼ cup vinegar
¼ cup olive oil
1 tablespoon lemon juice
Salt and pepper to taste
1 tablespoon chives, chopped
2 tablespoons parsley, minced for garnish

Boil potatoes in their jackets until tender.

Meanwhile, combine all other ingredients except chives and parsley and bring to a boil.

Cool potatoes slightly and peel. Slice thin and toss with hot dressing and chives. Cover with foil and put in 475° F. oven until thoroughly reheated.

Just before serving, toss again and garnish with minced parsley.

MINTED CUCUMBERS

SERVES 4–6

3 cucumbers, sliced
½ cup yogurt
2 teaspoons fresh mint, chopped

Combine all ingredients and chill before serving.

Tip: There should never be so much dressing that there is a puddle of it in the bottom of the salad bowl—whether the bowl is communal or individual.

After you have tossed the salad, if you suspect there is too much dressing, gently lift some of the salad away from the bottom of one side of the bowl and tip the bowl. If there is any liquid on the bottom, transfer the salad gently into a colander and then into a fresh bowl—or, if you have used your prize salad bowl to begin with, wipe it out with a paper towel and put the salad back in.

When adding dressing and tossing at the table, start with two tablespoons of whatever you are using and add more if necessary. It takes very little dressing to complete most salads.

CHEESE BALLS

3-ounce package cream cheese
¼ teaspoon honey

2 tablespoons raw beets, grated
½ teaspoon gelatin
1 tablespoon cold water
2 tablespoons unsalted raw peanuts, chopped fine

Mash cheese with honey until smooth and blend with beets.

Dissolve gelatin in cold water and blend into cheese mixture. Let set in refrigerator.

To serve, form chilled cheese into balls with melon scoop or teaspoon and roll in peanuts.

Serving suggestion: Use as a garnish on individual tossed green salads.

Tip: Tossed salads should be dealt with gently. The object is to blend the greens with the other ingredients and with the dressing without bruising the leaves. A light touch is needed.

SPRING IS GREEN

Like all simple ideas, this one is nearly perfect. It is refreshing, low in calories, gives people something unexpected to do, and is a special treat because it is available only to those so fortunate as to have peas in their garden, and even to them it is a treat for a very short season.

Just before a cocktail party, pick as many bowlfuls of peas as you think you will need—according to the size of your party.

Wash and dry, without removing them from the pods.

Fill bowls with these tender new peas and set out empty bowls alongside. Guests can help themselves to the raw peas, discarding the pods in the empty bowls.

Beats potato chips every time!

COTTAGE CHEESE CALCUTTA

Keep this recipe handy. You'll be asked for it every time you serve it.

SERVES 4–6

> ¼ cup butter
> ½ teaspoon fresh ginger, minced
> ¼ teaspoon coriander
> ¼ teaspoon turmeric
> ¼ teaspoon ground red chilies
> 8 ounces cottage cheese, preferably small curd
> 1 pound cooked peas (not canned)
> 4 tomatoes, cut in eighths
> Salt, to taste

Melt butter and add ginger, coriander, turmeric, and chilies. Cook, but do not allow butter to foam, for 2 to 3 minutes, stirring occasionally.

Cool to lukewarm—the butter should still be liquid. Meanwhile combine cottage cheese, peas, and tomatoes. Blend in liquid butter mixture and salt and stir gently but thoroughly. Chill.

POTATO SALAD WITH SOUR CREAM

> 1 cup sour cream
> 2 tablespoons vinegar
> 1 cup celery, chopped
> ½ cup cucumber, sliced
> ¼ teaspoon dry mustard
> Salt and pepper, to taste
> 2 tablespoons dill, minced
> 6 potatoes, cooked and sliced

Combine all ingredients, except the potatoes, leaving enough dill for garnish. Blend thoroughly.

Toss with potatoes and chill. Garnish with reserved dill just before serving.

TOMATO CHUTNEY

2 cups cider vinegar
4 garlic cloves, crushed
8 thin slices fresh ginger
2 green chili peppers
3 pounds tomatoes
2 small onions, chopped
2 pounds sugar
Salt, to taste

Put vinegar, garlic, ginger, and chili peppers in blender and reduce to liquid.

Scald tomatoes and peel. Boil tomatoes and onions in vinegar mixture 15 minutes. Add sugar, and salt to taste. Simmer until mixture reaches the consistency of chutney. (Allow for the fact that it will thicken as it cools.)

Can be kept in sterilized, sealed bottles or refrigerated.

SPANISH RICE

SERVES 4

2 cups cooked rice
1 garlic clove, minced
3 tablespoons Italian parsley, chopped
2 onions, minced

1 teaspoon turmeric
½ cup olive oil
3 tablespoons wine vinegar
Salt and pepper, to taste
6 tomatoes, sliced
3 hard-cooked eggs, chopped
2 Lemon Cucumbers, sliced
2 red peppers, julienne
2 tablespoons fresh dill, minced

Combine rice, garlic, parsley, onions, and turmeric in bowl. Toss with oil and vinegar and add salt and pepper to taste.

Place in a mound on a serving dish and arrange tomatoes, eggs, cucumbers, and peppers attractively in a ring around the rice. Sprinkle dill over rice and bring to the table.

PICKLED SHRIMP

2 pounds small cooked shrimp
2 onions, sliced in thin rings
1½ cups olive oil
1½ cups wine vinegar
¼ cup sugar
1 garlic clove, crushed
5 slices celeriac, minced
4 tablespoons capers
½ tablespoon tarragon, minced
1½ teaspoons salt

Chill shrimp. Layer shrimp and onions in jar. Combine all other ingredients and pour over shrimp. Cover tightly and marinate overnight. Drain (reserving marinade for another use) and serve.

GARLIC OLIVES
An interesting way to serve an old favorite.

1 can large black olives
1 garlic clove, minced
4 tablespoons olive oil
½ teaspoon salt

Combine all ingredients in a jar and shake gently to coat olives. Do not refrigerate.

Marinate for at least 24 hours, shaking occasionally to keep olives moist with oil.

Drain and serve.

GUACAMOLE
Equally good as a dip with corn chips, or as an appetizer.

MAKES ABOUT 1 CUP

1 large ripe avocado
2 tablespoons lemon juice
3 drops Tabasco sauce
½ small onion, minced
1 teaspoon garlic salt

Combine all ingredients, mashing the avocado to a smooth consistency.

Serving suggestion: If served as an appetizer, arrange a heaping tablespoonful of shredded lettuce, and garnish with a tomato wedge and two large black olives.

YANKEE COLESLAW

Nice for those who don't like mayonnaise or can't eat it because they are allergic to eggs.

SERVES 4–6

6 cups cabbage, shredded
¼ cup green pepper, diced
¼ cup red pepper, diced
½ teaspoon paprika
½ cup vinaigrette No. 1 dressing (see recipe page 174)
Salt, if needed

Combine all ingredients and chill thoroughly.

Tip: Always dry salad greens thoroughly before adding dressing. Use paper towels, salad basket, or just lay out on a large flat plate for an hour or so. If you have to choose between having your greens dry or chilled, choose dry every time.

HOLIDAY COLESLAW

To serve with cold turkey after Thanksgiving.

4 cups cabbage, shredded
2 cups apples, cored, seeded, and diced, but not peeled
1 cup cranberries, chopped
½ cup crushed pineapple, in natural juice
1 cup mayonnaise, thinned with a little cream
Salt and pepper, to taste
Paprika

Combine all ingredients, except paprika, and chill thoroughly. Garnish with a dusting of paprika.

CARROT RELISH

8 small carrots
12 shallots
1 tablespoon dill
1 cup cider vinegar
1 garlic clove, minced
½ cup water
1 tablespoon pickling spices

Scrape and slice carrots and cook in boiling salted water 5 minutes. Cool.

Peel shallots and slice.

Combine all remaining ingredients and simmer for 10 minutes. Pour over carrots and shallots. Cover tightly, refrigerate, and do not serve for 2 weeks.

BROCCOLI-CHICKEN MOUSSE

SERVES 6

2 cups cooked chicken, chopped
2 cups cooked broccoli, chopped
½ cup mayonnaise
2 tablespoons lemon juice
2 tablespoons Worcestershire sauce
¼ teaspoon cayenne pepper
1½ tablespoons gelatin
½ cup chicken stock
¾ cup heavy cream, whipped

Blend chicken, broccoli, mayonnaise, lemon juice, Worcestershire sauce, and cayenne pepper at low speed in blender.

Soften gelatin in chicken stock for 5 minutes, then dissolve over hot water.

Fold chicken mixture into whipped cream. Fold in gelatin. Pour into 1½-quart mold and chill until firm. Unmold and serve with Green Goddess dressing (see recipe page 165) on the side.

CRANBERRY-CHICKEN MOLD

SERVES 6

2½ cups cranberry juice
2 teaspoons orange juice
2 teaspoons agar-agar
4 celery stalks, chopped fine
2 cups boiled chicken, in chunks
6 hard-cooked eggs, chopped
½ cup mayonnaise
Watercress, for garnish

Combine cranberry juice and orange juice in saucepan and bring to a boil. Add agar-agar, beating in with a wire whisk. Continue whisking for 3 minutes. Remove from heat and allow to cool. Meanwhile put celery, chicken, and eggs in 1½-quart chilled mold. Pour in cranberry mixture. When room temperature, place in refrigerator until set—about 3 hours.

Unmold and serve with mayonnaise. Garnish with greens— watercress is especially nice.

Note: Agar-agar is available in Oriental and health food stores. It is a natural product made from seaweed, is easy to use instead of gelatin, and is considered very good for you. It makes delicious candies, molds, and desserts.

To Pickle Cucumbers

Let your cucumbers be small, fresh gathered, and free from spots; then make a pickle of salt and water, strong enough to bear an egg; boil the pickle and skim it well, and then pour it upon the cucumbers, and stive them down for twenty four hours; then drain them out into a cullender, and dry them well with a cloth, and take the best white wine vinegar, with cloves, sliced mace, nutmeg, white pepper corns, long pepper, and races of ginger (as much as you please) boil them up together, and then clap the cucumbers in, with a few vine leaves, and a little salt, and as soon as they begin to turn their colour, put them into jars, stive them down close, and when cold, tie on a bladder and leather.

From an eighteenth-century American cookbook.

CHAPTER ELEVEN

Salad Sauces and Dressings

THE SIMPLEST SALAD can be a gourmet dish if properly sauced or dressed—and the finest ingredients can be reduced to complete boredom by an indifferent dressing. The basic rules are easy: do not use a sweet dressing with salads unless they have fruit in them; and do not use too spicy a dressing with delicately flavored ingredients.

Remember also that no recipe is inviolate; you can always spice it up or down according to your taste without changing its basic character.

CHICKPEA DRESSING
A tasty way to add protein to a vegetable salad.

1 cup cooked chickpeas
1 cup sour cream
2 garlic cloves, minced

3 tablespoons cider vinegar
¼ teaspoon cayenne
Salt and pepper, to taste

Put all ingredients in blender and blend until perfectly smooth. If too thick, add a little more sour cream and vinegar.

GREEN GODDESS

This salad dressing was invented in California in the early twentieth century, in honor of George Arliss, who was starring in a play by that name. Although not many people today would remember the play, the fame of this dressing lives on.

1 cup mayonnaise
1 garlic clove, crushed
1 tablespoon fresh chives, chopped
4 scallions, sliced thin
⅓ cup parsley, minced
⅓ cup sour cream
2 tablespoons tarragon vinegar
Salt and pepper, to taste

Put all ingredients in blender and blend until smooth—it shouldn't take more than a few seconds.

MINT DRESSING

4 tablespoons lemon juice
2 tablespoons honey
5 tablespoons peanut oil
2 tablespoons sesame oil
4 tablespoons fresh mint, chopped
Salt and pepper, to taste

Combine all ingredients and whisk until blended.

SAUCE DIJON
Delicious spooned over cold roast meats.

> 6 shallots, minced
> 6 tablespoons French olive oil
> 1 tablespoon flour
> 1 tablespoon chicken broth
> 3 tablespoons white wine
> 1 cup mushrooms, chopped
> 1/4 teaspoon parsley, minced
> 1/4 teaspoon chervil, minced
> 1/4 teaspoon basil, minced
> 1/4 teaspoon Dijon mustard
> Salt and pepper, to taste
> 2 tablespoons lemon juice

Sauté shallots in oil until golden. Sprinkle with flour and stir to mix. Add chicken broth and stir. Add all other ingredients, except lemon juice, and simmer slowly for 15 minutes. Cool, then add lemon juice.

YOGURT DRESSING FOR YOUR FAVORITE POTATO SALAD
If you usually use mayonnaise, try this instead.

> 2 cups yogurt
> 1 cup heavy cream, whipped
> 2 tablespoons onions, chopped
> 1 tablespoon dill, minced
> 3 tablespoons Italian parsley, minced
> 2 tablespoons cider vinegar
> Salt and pepper, to taste

Combine yogurt and cream. Add all other ingredients, stirring gently to mix. Add to your potato salad and toss.

Chill thoroughly.

SAUCE NIÇOISE

For fish salad plates.

> 2 tomatoes, chopped
> 1 green pepper, chopped fine
> 1 garlic clove, minced
> ½ onion, minced
> 1 tablespoon capers
> 1 teaspoon olive oil
> 1 teaspoon lemon juice
> ¼ teaspoon fresh tarragon, minced
> Salt and pepper, to taste

Combine all ingredients and spoon over fish.

HORSERADISH SAUCE

For shrimp salad plates, use with discretion or make a milder version.

> 1 cup mayonnaise
> 1 teaspoon fresh horseradish, grated
> 1 tablespoon cider vinegar
> 2 tablespoons capers
> Salt and pepper, to taste

Mix all ingredients just before serving.

TAHINI

¼ cup tahini
2 teaspoons soy sauce
2 slices fresh ginger, grated
2 tablespoons sesame oil
2 tablespoons rice vinegar
1 teaspoon dry mustard
Salt, if needed

Combine all ingredients and stir until smooth and well blended.

Serving suggestion: For dip, thicken with sour cream.

Note: Tahini is sesame seed paste and is available in Chinese or health food markets. Before using, stir to combine paste and oil, which will have separated and floated to the top.

CURRIED SOUR CREAM DRESSING

1 cup sour cream
1 teaspoon curry
¼ teaspoon cumin
¼ teaspoon cayenne
1 garlic clove, minced

Blend all ingredients thoroughly and chill before serving.

PINK MAYONNAISE
Attractive with vegetable salads when you want a bit of extra color.

    1 cup mayonnaise
    Enough beet juice to give the color you want

Blend and chill. The beet juice can be saved from canned beets. (If you wish, you can blend in a tablespoon of chopped cooked beets or grated raw beets as well.)

ROQUEFORT DRESSING
I love Roquefort but I do not like the Roquefort dressings that are smooth and white. This is my favorite kind.

    ½ cup vinaigrette No. 1 dressing (see recipe page 173)
    ¼ cup Roquefort cheese, crumbled

Combine but do not beat—the cheese should be in recognizable crumbles.

SALAD TARTARE SAUCE
An adaptation of the traditional sauce tartare served with fried fish. This works especially well with fish salads and can be used instead of mayonnaise in a mold or mousse, but then it must be thickened to the consistency of mayonnaise by reducing the liquid in the mousse recipe.

    1 cup mayonnaise
    2 tablespoons cider vinegar
    1 teaspoon dry mustard

2 tablespoons sweet pickles, chopped
1 tablespoon capers, chopped
1 tablespoon shallots, chopped
2 tablespoons Italian parsley, chopped
Salt and pepper, to taste

Blend mayonnaise with vinegar and mustard. Combine with all other ingredients.

SOUR CREAM FRUIT DRESSING

½ cup sour cream
3 tablespoons orange juice
1 teaspoon orange rind, grated
1 teaspoon lemon rind, grated
1 teaspoon lemon juice
Salt, to taste

Blend all ingredients thoroughly.

WALNUT SAUCE

3 garlic cloves, minced
1 small chili pepper, minced
2 pounds walnuts, chopped
Salt, to taste
3 tablespoons olive oil
½ teaspoon sesame oil

Combine all ingredients except the oils in mortar and grind to a smooth paste.

Combine the oils and add slowly, beating steadily, as if making mayonnaise by hand, until paste takes on consistency of sauce.

Serving suggestions: Excellent with platter of cold roast veal; as a spread for hors d'oeuvre topped with a slice of hard-cooked egg sprinkled with paprika; or mixed with cottage cheese as a dip for crudités.

YOGURT DRESSING

1 cup plain yogurt
½ cup safflower oil
½ cup cider vinegar
Salt and pepper, to taste

Blend all ingredients thoroughly. Chill until ready to serve. Shake just before pouring over salad.

YOGURT DRESSING FOR FRUIT SALADS

1 cup plain yogurt
½ cup safflower oil
½ teaspoon sesame oil
¼ teaspoon cardamom
2 tablespoons orange juice
1 teaspoon pineapple juice
Salt and pepper, to taste

Blend all ingredients thoroughly. Chill until ready to serve. Shake just before pouring over salad.

YOGURT DRESSING FOR COLD ROAST VEAL

1 cup plain yogurt
½ cup safflower oil
½ teaspoon thyme
½ teaspoon garlic, minced
¼ cup cider vinegar
Salt and pepper, to taste

Blend all ingredients thoroughly. Chill until ready to serve. Shake just before using.

SPINACH GREEN FOR COLOURING VARIOUS DISHES
Ingredients—2 handfuls of spinach.
Mode—Pick and wash the spinach free from dirt, and pound the leaves in a mortar to extract the juice; then press it through a hair sieve, and put the juice into a small stewpan or jar. Place this in a bain marie, or saucepan of boiling water, and let it set. Watch it closely, as it should not boil; and, as soon as it is done, lay it in a sieve, so that all the water may drain from it, and the green will then be ready for colouring.

From Mrs. Beeton's *Book of Household Management,* 1861.

CHINOISE DRESSING

2 tablespoons peanut oil
1 tablespoon sesame oil
2 tablespoons cider vinegar
1 tablespoon rice vinegar

1 tablespoon soy sauce
½ teaspoon fresh ginger, grated
Salt, to taste

Thoroughly blend all ingredients except salt. Add salt only if
desired after tasting.

PINEAPPLE MAYONNAISE

1 egg
2 tablespoons vinegar
½ teaspoon dry mustard
¼ teaspoon salt
1 cup olive oil
¼ teaspoon crème de menthe
⅓ cup crushed pineapple, well drained
6 fresh mint leaves, minced

In blender, put whole egg (minus the shell, of course) . Add
vinegar, mustard, salt, ¼ cup of olive oil, and crème de menthe.

Blend on low speed, and as it blends, add rest of olive oil in
steady stream. After about 15 seconds, blend on high for a few
seconds.

Remove mayonnaise from blender and add pineapple and
mint leaves. Blend thoroughly and chill until needed.

VINAIGRETTE
*Like all classic recipes, this basic French dressing comes in many
variations. It takes its name from the small bottle in which
salad dressings were often served, so obviously the first recipes
did not call for any solid ingredients that could not pass through*

the tiny perforated top. Here are two recipes—one probably the original, one a later variation. I add garlic to both, but theoretically you shouldn't.

VINAIGRETTE NO. 1

> 2 tablespoons French olive oil
> 1 tablespoon wine vinegar
> 1 teaspoon dry mustard
> Salt and pepper, to taste

Combine all ingredients, shake or stir briskly, and pour over salad. That's all there is to it. I like to add 1 tablespoon of lemon juice, but that is not traditional and gives it the wrong proportion of oil to vinegar for classic French vinaigrette. Try it both ways and decide for yourself.

VINAIGRETTE NO. 2

To the above recipe add:

> 1 tablespoon capers, drained and chopped
> 1 tablespoon chives, chopped
> 1/4 teaspoon chervil
> 1/2 cup Italian parsley, minced
> 1/4 teaspoon tarragon

Combine all ingredients, shake briskly, and pour over salad. If you add any other ingredients, you are making something that is possibly very interesting—but not a true vinaigrette.

SAUCE VERTE

Don't confuse this with the green sauce you get on clams and other shellfish in Spanish restaurants. This is a seasoned mayonnaise.

1 teaspoon chervil
1 tablespoon fresh tarragon, minced
1 teaspoon dill
2 tablespoons chives, minced
1½ cups mayonnaise

Pound herbs in mortar to a paste and blend into mayonnaise.

AÏOLI

*The grandmother of mayonnaise, and one taste of it is enough
to make you think we're much bigger sissies than grandmother
ever was—it's traditionally loaded with garlic. This is a milder
version.*

1 egg
2 garlic cloves, minced
2 tablespoons wine vinegar
Salt and pepper, to taste
1 cup French olive oil

Put egg, garlic, vinegar, salt, pepper, and ¼ cup of oil in
blender and put on high speed. Quickly add remaining olive
oil in steady stream.

If you are an absolute purist, omit the vinegar and beat together all the ingredients except the oil. Then continue beating
while you add the oil very, very slowly.

*Garlicks, tho' used by the French, are better adapted
to the use of medicine than cookery.*
From an eighteenth-century American cookbook.

APPENDIXES

SEED CATALOG SOURCES

There are many more good seedsmen than those listed below; this is just my personal list.

Burpee Seeds
W. Atlee Burpee Co.
Warminster, Pa. 18974

Burrell Seed Growers Co.
Rocky Ford Seed House
Rocky Ford, Colo. 81067

J. A. Demonchaux Co., Inc.,
   Importers
225 Jackson
Topeka, Kansas 66603

Henry Field Seed & Nursery Co.
Shenandoah, Iowa 51602

Gurney's Seed & Nursery Co.
Yankton, S.D. 57078

Joseph Harris Co., Inc.
Moreton Farm
Rochester, N.Y. 14624

Le Jardin du Gourmet
Les Eschalottes
Ramsey, N.J. 07446

Nichols Garden Nursery
1190 North Pacific Highway
Albany, Oregon 97321

Stokes Seeds, Inc.
Box 548
Buffalo, N.Y. 14240

Thompson & Morgan, Inc.
P.O. Box 24
401 Kennedy Boulevard
Somerdale, N.J. 08083

SOURCES OF ORGANIC FERTILIZERS

Fertilizer	Sources
BORON	Granite dust, clover, vetch, muskmelon leaves
CALCIUM	Wood ash, limestone, bonemeal, eggshells, seashells
COBALT	Manure, compost, Kentucky bluegrass, most legume refuse, peach tree leaves
COPPER	Dandelion leaves, sawdust, Kentucky bluegrass, wood shavings
IRON	Seaweed, fish emulsion, manure, dried blood
MANGANESE	Limestone, hickory and white oak leaves, carrot tops, alfalfa
MOLYBDENUM	Rock phosphate, alfalfa, vetch
NITROGEN	Chicken manure, fish meal, dried blood, snow, cottonseed meal, soybean meal
PHOSPHORUS	Fish meal, bonemeal, rock phosphate, eggshells, seashells
POTASSIUM	Seaweed, citrus peel, melon rind, greensand, granite dust, sheep, horse & pig manure, wood ash
ZINC	Manure, poplar and hickory leaves, cornstalks, peach tree leaves, vetch

Note: A well-made compost heap will provide almost all of the fertilizers you need for your vegetable garden.

SEED PLANTING CHART

ALL MEASUREMENTS IN INCHES

Vegetable	Depth to Plant Seed	Distance Between Seeds	Distance Between Rows
Anise	¼	8–12	12
Belgian Endive	¼	7–8	18
Cabbage	½	Spring: 12–18	
		Fall: 18–30	24
Carrot	¼	1½	12–14
Celery	⅛	8	24–28
Chicory	½	12	12–24
Chinese Cabbage	½	10–18	24–30
Cucumber	1	5–6 per hill, 2" apart	48–72
Dill	¼	6–8	9
Escarole	½	12	12–24
Florence Fennel	1	8	18
Lettuce, head	¼–½	12	18
Lettuce, leaf	¼	6	12
Parsley	¼	3–6	12–24

Vegetable	Depth to Plant Seed	Distance Between Seeds	Distance Between Rows
Pepper	¼	18–24	24–36
Radish	½	1–3	6–12
Spinach	½	4–6	12–18
Summer Spinach—Malabar	½	12	12
Summer Spinach—New Zealand	1–1½	18	24
Summer Spinach—Tampala	¼–½	4–6	24
Tomatoes	½	18–36	36–60
Watercress	¼	1	–

STATE AGRICULTURAL
EXPERIMENT STATIONS

ALABAMA   Cooperative Extension Service
Auburn University
Auburn 36830

ALASKA   Agricultural Experiment Station
University of Alaska
College 99701

ARIZONA   Cooperative Extension Service
University of Arizona
College of Agriculture
Tucson 85721

ARKANSAS	Cooperative Extension Service University of Arkansas Fayetteville 72701
CALIFORNIA	Agricultural Extension Service University of California College of Agriculture Berkeley 94720
COLORADO	Cooperative Extension Service Colorado State University Fort Collins 80521
CONNECTICUT	Cooperative Extension Service University of Connecticut College of Agriculture & Natural Resources Storrs 06268
DELAWARE	Cooperative Extension Service University of Delaware College of Agricultural Sciences Newark 19711
DISTRICT OF COLUMBIA	Cooperative Extension Service The Federal City College 1424 K Street, N.W. Washington, D.C. 20005
FLORIDA	Cooperative Extension Service University of Florida Institute of Food & Agricultural Sciences Gainesville 32601
GEORGIA	Cooperative Extension Service University of Georgia College of Agriculture Athens 30601
HAWAII	Agricultural Extension Service University of Hawaii Honolulu 96822

IDAHO	Cooperative Extension Service University of Idaho College of Agriculture Moscow 83843
ILLINOIS	Cooperative Extension Service University of Illinois College of Agriculture Urbana 61801
INDIANA	Cooperative Extension Service Purdue University West Lafayette 47907
IOWA	Cooperative Extension Service Iowa State University Ames 50010
KANSAS	Cooperative Extension Service Kansas State University College of Agriculture Manhattan 66502
KENTUCKY	Cooperative Extension Service University of Kansas College of Agriculture Lexington 40506
LOUISIANA	Agricultural Experiment Station Louisiana State University Agricultural College Baton Rouge 70800
MAINE	Cooperative Extension Service University of Maine College of Agriculture Orono 04473
MARYLAND	Cooperative Extension Service University of Maryland College Park 20740

MASSACHUSETTS	Cooperative Extension Service University of Massachusetts College of Agriculture Amherst 01002
MICHIGAN	Cooperative Extension Service Michigan State University College of Agriculture East Lansing 48823
MINNESOTA	Agricultural Extension Service University of Minnesota Institute of Agriculture St. Paul 55101
MISSISSIPPI	Cooperative Extension Service Mississippi State University State College 39762
MISSOURI	Cooperative Extension Service University of Missouri College of Agriculture Columbia 65201
MONTANA	Cooperative Extension Service Montana State University Bozeman 59715
NEBRASKA	Cooperative Extension Service University of Nebraska College of Agriculture & Home Economics Lincoln 68503
NEVADA	Cooperative Extension Service University of Nevada College of Agriculture Reno 89507
NEW HAMPSHIRE	Cooperative Extension Service University of New Hampshire College of Life Sciences & Agriculture Durham 03824

NEW JERSEY   Cooperative Extension Service
Rutgers
College of Agriculture & Environmental Sciences
New Brunswick 08903

NEW MEXICO   Cooperative Extension Service
New Mexico State University
Box 3AE, Agriculture Building
Las Cruces 88003

NEW YORK   Cooperative Extension Service
Cornell University
College of Agriculture
Ithaca 14850

NORTH CAROLINA   Cooperative Extension Service
North Carolina State University
P.O. Box 5157
Raleigh 27607

NORTH DAKOTA   Cooperative Extension Service
North Dakota State University of Agriculture
& Applied Science
University Station
Fargo 58102

OHIO   Cooperative Extension Service
Ohio State University
Agriculture Administration Building
2120 Fyffe Road
Columbus 43210

OKLAHOMA   Cooperative Extension Service
Oklahoma State University
201 Whitehurst
Stillwater 74074

OREGON   Cooperative Extension Service
Oregon State University
Corvallis 97331

PENNSYLVANIA Cooperative Extension Service
Pennsylvania State University
College of Agriculture
323 Agricultural Administration Building
University Park 16802

RHODE ISLAND Cooperative Extension Service
University of Rhode Island
Kingston 02881

SOUTH CAROLINA Cooperative Extension Service
Clemson University
Clemson 29631

SOUTH DAKOTA Cooperative Extension Service
South Dakota State University
College of Agriculture
Brookings 57006

TENNESSEE Agricultural Extension Service
University of Tennessee
Institute of Agriculture
P.O. Box 1071
Knoxville 37901

TEXAS Agricultural Extension Service
Texas A & M University
College Station 77483

UTAH Cooperative Extension Service
Utah State University
College of Agriculture
Logan 84321

VERMONT Cooperative Extension Service
University of Vermont
State Agricultural College
Burlington 05401

VIRGINIA	Cooperative Extension Service Virginia Polytechnic Institute Blacksburg 24061
WASHINGTON	Cooperative Extension Service Washington State University College of Agriculture Pullman 99163
WEST VIRGINIA	Cooperative Extension Service West Virginia University Morgantown 26506
WISCONSIN	Cooperative Extension Service University of Wisconsin College of Agriculture 432 North Lake Street Madison 53706
WYOMING	Agricultural Extension Service University of Wyoming University Station Box 3354 Laramie 82070

Gardening Index

Recipe Index

GERI HARRINGTON

GERI HARRINGTON *lives in Wilton, Connecticut, where, when she is not growing vegetables and turning them into delectable salads, she runs an advertising agency with her husband.*